To Sweden with love

First published by Augusta Press 2020
augustapress.com

© Graham Shearwood 2020

Disclaimer: The personal stories and memories by individuals recorded here are their versions of events and have been provided and reproduced in good faith with no disrespect or defamation intended. Some names have been changed to protect the privacy of individuals.

All rights reserved. This book or any portion thereof may not be reproduced or used in any manner whatsoever without the express written permission of the publisher except for the use of brief quotations in a book review.

ISBN 978-0-6489409-0-6 (paperback)
ISBN 978-0-6489409-1-3 (eBook)

Cover and text design: Helen Shearwood / helenshearwood.com
Consultancy: Pickawoowoo Publishing Group / pickawoowoo.com
Printed and distributed by Ingram (Aus/USA/UK/EUR)

A catalogue record for this work is available from the National Library of Australia

To Sweden with love
Memories from the 1970s

Graham Shearwood

Augusta Press

For Wendy, Helen and Martin

*And Helena, who gave us a glimpse
of what it is to be Swedish
and who inspired our daughter's name*

Contents

Prelude

Part 1 – 1971 Stockholm   1

  1. The road to Stockholm   3
  2. Faraway places: Farsta and Hägersten   19
  3. LM Ericsson   27
  4. Helena   37
  5. A week in Czechoslovakia   43
  6. Summer with Belle   61
  7. Midsummer in Dalarna   69
  8. The end of the summer   75
  9. Helsinki weekend   91
  10. Christmas in London   95

Part 2 – 1972-73 Droppsta   99

  11. Down and out in Paris   101
  12. Not so Dynamic Data   108
  13. Burroughs   123
  14. Droppsta   134

Postscript   153

To our friends in Sweden   161

Prelude

This is the story of a chapter in my life – the time Wendy and I spent living and working in Sweden from January 1971 to April 1973. The main purpose of the story is to give our children, Helen and Martin, a taste of a period in our lives that they have no experience of. If other people read it and enjoy it, then that's a bonus. I also felt a strong need to put down in words something that will survive me.

Why just this one period? Well, the thought of writing about my whole life was just too daunting – both for me and no doubt for any reader. These particular years were exciting for us, and also a change of culture. So I hope that puts a sharper focus on us than time spent in our own country.

These events happened fifty years ago, a fact which is hard for us to believe now. Even after such a long time, between the two of us we remember the main parts of the story and we have some vivid memories of those days. Some details, it must be said, elude us both; and that makes us wonder how a particular episode did actually play out. But it did happen, I can promise you.

My brother Ian was a fresh pair of eyes on an early draft of this book and saw things that I didn't see. The result is the better for his insight and I thank him for that.

I thank our daughter Helen for her design of this book, both text and covers. You dear Helen are brilliant at making things look just right, among your many other talents.

Our son Martin was the inspiration that led to us finding our stuga in Blekinge in later years. I thank you for that Martin, and for sharing that memorable journey of exploration and discovery.

I thank Wendy more than words can say; both for playing a starring role in this drama, and for helping me re-live it fifty years later.

Graham Shearwood
Augusta, Western Australia
2020

Part 1

1971 Stockholm

1

The road to Stockholm

It was Thursday January 7th 1971. I still remember the date after all these years. Maybe not so surprising as it was a big adventure in our young lives – I was 23 and Wendy 22. We had left Nottingham and were heading for Tilbury in the south-east of England in our blue Mini, containing many of our worldly possessions, to catch the ferry to Gothenburg and our new life in Stockholm.

Let's quickly go back a year and a half to June 1969. The swinging sixties were at an end. I had been living in Nottingham since going there to university to do Maths. (That was a mistake: I should have done Modern Languages.) Those three years could not have been more exhilarating. In my first year I'd been quite diligent – probably because the habits of school education had not yet worn off. But in the second and third years things got a bit ragged – lectures were skipped, course projects went undone, and extracurricular activities increased. Regrets? – some but not many. The things that I did do also came under the heading of education. But you couldn't stay a student for ever: it was a protected, privileged, unsustainable way of life.

So when the Finals results were pinned on the board and I saw I'd got a Third (the lowest grade), was I disappointed? No, I was elated: my three years had not been in vain academically. I could have done better if I'd studied more – but doesn't everybody who doesn't get a First say that? The main thing was that I was a Bachelor of Science (with Honours, even), and it was something to put on my CV.

Now, all of a sudden, at the age of twenty-two, I was about to enter the real world. No more grant cheques. A bank account deeply in the red. I desperately needed an income, and that, I realised, meant getting a job.

I'd had a temporary job in a scientific company during my gap year, where I'd been introduced to computer programming, and I really loved that. I thought, that's what I really want to do as a career, but all the programming jobs that were advertised in *Computer Weekly* – and there were pages and pages of them in all parts of the country – typically wanted twelve months of commercial programming experience. It was the same old story: it's hard to get your first job and your foot on the ladder.

A couple of months before graduating I'd seen an advert for a job at Nottingham City Treasury for a trainee systems analyst – what we'd now call a business analyst. It wasn't my ideal job, but it was in my home town, it was in the computer department, and it involved some connection with a computer. So I applied. And, as fate would have it, I got the job. I was very happy about that, because at least I would have some money coming in every month – about £90 in fact, or £1000 a year. Not a bad wage in those days: to give you an idea, my monthly rent on a three-bedroom flat in leafy West Bridgford was all of £16 a month. And that was sharing with someone else (more of that later).

Sadly, as I said, there was no money in the bank for a last summer fling on the beaches of Spain or for any other worldly pleasures, as some of my fellow graduates were able to afford. On that fateful day, July 7th 1969, I entered the workforce – having first invested in two business shirts and a haircut. There were other things happening in the world at large: two weeks later a man would walk on the moon.

As could have been foretold, I soon became unhappy in my job. There was too much business, and not much IT. I felt completely out of my depth as someone who had only known academic life, was very young, with no experience of business. Nor was I a local lad – I was one of those southerners. In this situation I could have talked things over with my manager. But, as was to be a recurring theme of my career, I didn't, and struggled on for a year and a half until I found a new job and was able, with great relief, to hand in my notice. While we're on the subject, a related failing of mine has been the search for perfection. Or should that 'has been' be 'is'? Did I just forget a comma? I've listened to the songs of Leonard Cohen all my life, and know them all. I should have heeded his words about cracks letting the light in.

All in all I was not in a good place when the 1970s dawned. I so missed the joy of student life. I even hated the music – something called punk – which to me was just a horrible noise, after all that incredibly beautiful music of the 1960s.

And then there was the huge overdraft at the bank from student days – several hundred pounds. The bank must have had faith in me, maybe because some money was now coming in, but I was making little if any progress in paying off my debts. Every month or so I'd get a letter from the bank. I didn't like to open it. But all my friendly bank manager wrote was words to the effect, 'We would be pleased to receive a credit, and we hope you are enjoying this beautiful weather.' I am forever grateful to the Midland Bank for their forbearance. (I still have the same account at the same branch in Nottingham. But sadly no longer called the Midland Bank.)

There was however one big plus to my new job: my best friend Wendy worked there. She it was who I shared the flat with. She had also fallen in love with programming (as I had with her), and she was sensible enough, after a year at university, to get a job doing just that. So Wendy was happy in her work, and had also made lots of friends (as she does).

Strangely enough, I hadn't yet met Wendy when I applied for the job. But now we were working at the same place. Not actually in the same office, but almost. We bumped into each other occasionally during the working day. I liked that. Sometimes we drove in to work in Wendy's Mini, and sometimes we caught the bus. We may even have shared an umbrella (as at the Hollies' bus stop).

I'd better tell you here a bit about how that all started. I was sharing with two lads in a block of flats in West Bridgford. One day from my eyrie on the fifth floor, I was struck by a vision of loveliness down below, with golden hair down to her waist. I was truly dazzled. It didn't take long to find out that this person lived on the second floor of this very block of flats. And it wasn't long either before we came face to face in the lift.

Some time towards the end of 1969, we had been going out for six months, and we were very happy together, but getting married wasn't even on the horizon. Wendy was a career girl with no thought of married life and all that that implied – housework, children, hubby with slippers to come home to, etc. She said that a generation earlier she would have been a Bletchley girl decoding secret messages, and doing cryptic crosswords when she had a spare moment. Wendy felt that as a woman you had to be better than all the rest if you were to succeed in the world of IT. And she was. So it was a surprise to her, and to me, when one day I asked her if she would marry me. 'Are you drunk?' she asked. Then, before I'd had time to reply, she said, 'Oh? Yes'. I was happy to hear that. It was as though she didn't intend to get married, but for me she would make an exception (as for Leonard in the Chelsea Hotel). And fifty years later we still have stars in our eyes.

But just a minute, I hear you say, 'you didn't have any money. Don't you have to save up to get married?' I have to say the thought never crossed my mind. Wendy, to her credit, didn't seem to mind either. Nor did her parents ever ask me about my 'prospects'.

But when would be the day? We both liked numbers, and the sixth of the sixth in the new decade seemed to have a certain ring about it, and it would be a Saturday, so we set the date for June 6th 1970. It meant there would be plenty of time to do whatever needed to be done.

And so it happened that we were married in St. Thomas's Church, Streatham Hill in London on a fine summer's day. I'd passed my driving test three days before, so I was able to drive away from the reception quite legally. Two weeks of blissful freedom lay ahead of us.

We drove down to Newhaven and got the ferry to Dieppe. Looking for the sun, we headed south through France, stopping at the most basic hotels in the Michelin

Guide – the ones with a wine glass with a roof over the top. We stayed in La Rochelle, Royan and Arcachon, getting towards the Spanish border. We spent many hours lying in the sun on French beaches – yes really – and got a bit sunburnt. We were happy though we didn't have much money. Maybe *because* we didn't have much money.

Some time after we got back from France, Wendy got a new job with more money at SPL (Systems Programming Ltd), a software house with an office in Nottingham. Those were the days when Information Technology was in its infancy and if you had a year or more's programming experience, you'd be considered an experienced professional and snapped up by a new employer and offered a huge pay rise.

SPL were a leading player in the industry in those days. They had branches in several European cities, mostly staffed by Brits. For some reason Brits were highly regarded in the industry at that time. Probably because the only training available then was directly from computer manufacturers, and they had offices in the UK more than in mainland Europe. And with English being the world's international language, much of the weighty printed documentation was only published in English.

SPL were looking for some likely people to work in Stockholm on a contract at LM Ericsson, even then a world player in the telecommunications industry. This was long before the age of the mobile phone and PCs, and at that time LM's main focus was the design and manufacture of telephones, and more relevantly for us, software-controlled telephone exchanges. Nowadays the company is better known simply as Ericsson.

We were both up for an adventure and eager to travel. Ever since I can remember I have loved exploring new places, even if it was just a new part of town in wherever I was living. When I was only seven, our family moved with Dad's job to a new town – Cheltenham in Gloucestershire. I immediately wanted to know what was down the street from where we were living, and then what was around the corner, and so on. So I jumped on my bike to find out. What's more, the human brain has this remarkable property that it remembers when you go somewhere new, so that if and when you go there again, it's more or less familiar. I love that. It's all to do with connecting neurons to synapses, I read somewhere.

So Wendy told her manager that her husband was also in IT and we would be happy to work on the Ericsson contract. I sent in my CV. It wasn't long before I found myself in the SPL office in Nottingham being interviewed. I'm not sure I was asked anything very taxing and the young manager gave my CV a cursory glance: 'Yes, this is what we're looking for', I remember him saying, 'Twelve months high-level programming experience, and twelve months assembler experience.'

Interesting maths, considering I'd only had a proper job for eighteen months, and that not in programming. But I didn't have any family ties and I had a bit of experience, and they offered me the job. I can still remember for how much: £1500 a year. A fifty percent pay rise – great. But also, if you were working abroad, you got living expenses on top of that, which were as much as the salary. Not unreasonable, as you had to rent accommodation in an expensive city, and the cost of living was a fair bit higher than in the UK. What was not to like? And there were two of us, so doubly good. Who cared if the beer in Sweden was said to cost five times what it did back home? The money was a nice bonus which helped after many months to turn my bank balance from red to black, but it was the adventure that lured us both.

We had each spent some holidays on mainland Europe, in France and Spain mostly, but we had never been to Scandinavia before. Although, by another strange coincidence, we had earlier booked a week's holiday in May 1971 in a log cabin deep in the Swedish countryside. That only confirmed it was the right move for us. We were going with another couple who also happened to live in Nottingham and were both in IT. She was working for SPL also, and they had applied for the Ericsson contract too – but they had been knocked back. Were they mad at us? Maybe they were, but they never said anything to us, which was nice of them. (And we did go ahead with the week in the log cabin, with our friends. We only had to drive from Stockholm, and they got the ferry over from England. We had a great holiday together – but let's not get ahead of ourselves.)

What was I expecting of our new home? Well, I loved what I'd seen of Swedish design. Not that IKEA was a concept known in Britain at that time, although we were to find out it was already successful over there. (Another unknown concept was ABBA: they wouldn't be known to the world for another three years.)

And I knew it was a large empty country with lots of pine forests and they made Volvos. I also admired their progressive social attitudes, which you often read about in the UK media. I'd also seen some of Ingmar Bergman's films, which were very different from most movies of the time, and they made a huge impression on me. Also some of Bo Widerberg's films, in particular *Elvira Madigan* with its vivid colours of stunning Danish landscapes. What a breathtaking sensual pleasure that was when you're in the middle of a grey wet English winter. (No doubt Danish winters are just as grey and wet, but let that pass.) That film made such an impact on me that I had to go and see it again the following night. In short, I was already in love with Scandinavia before I'd even set foot on its soil and I knew I was going to love being there. Starry-eyed? Oh yes.

So, to resume our story, on that happy Thursday, with the Christmas turkey barely cold, we rolled into Tilbury, a large commercial port on the north bank of the Thames. We wove our way through the myriad wharves with container ships everywhere and eventually found our ship at the Swedish Lloyd berth. Here was the vessel that was going to take us to a new world and a new life and excitement. It sailed early evening and it took thirty-six hours to get to Gothenburg, across the North Sea. Two nights and the day in between.

We'd been able to book a good cabin – an outside two-berth on the upper deck. So, a real porthole, with a view of the sky and sea. A luxury we wouldn't (couldn't) have allowed ourselves if our employer hadn't been paying. And it was a taste of things to come, in that the cabin – in fact the whole ship – was so stylish. Scandinavian in fact.

Soon it was time for a bite to eat. We went down to the restaurant and it turned out to be a real genuine *smörgåsbord* – and what an inviting spread. We'd never seen a proper *smörgåsbord* before. And, what's more, drinks were included. Amongst those on offer were different types of aquavit, the powerful and delicious Swedish snaps, distilled from grain and potatoes, and flavoured with a variety of herbs. That was no doubt a good incentive for attracting Swedish customers. There weren't many English passengers, that was clear. That was our first taste of aquavit – and we loved it (and still do). Also our first taste of sill (pickled herring), marinated in so many different ways. We were hooked from the first bite (as were the herring). What a feast that was. Several years later we did the same trip again and the food was as good as before, although the drinks were no longer included.

Friday morning dawned cold and bright. The sea was dead calm with hardly a ripple. The day passed in a relaxed sort of way, with a meal here and there. And now and then a smoke (of tobacco). We noticed a lot of people were smoking a brand of cigarette called Prince, from a distinctive red and white packet (no restrictions on toxic fumes then). So we had to try some of those. And they tasted good, too good you could say. We were to puff our way through quite a few packets of Prince in the following months (but not years).

By mid-afternoon the light started to fade: we were heading steadily north. An announcement was made that there would be bingo in one of the lounges. We'd never really played that before, so we had to have a go. There were quite a few punters in the comfortable bar area. We got our card and somebody called the numbers out, in Swedish and English. Almost every number that came up, we'd got on our card. Hey this game's easy. The tension. Then – our last number comes up, 'Bingo!' They must have thought we'd made a mistake, we were so early, but we hadn't, we'd won a prize! Wendy even remembers what we won – a voucher for the ship's shop, where she bought some cosmetics by LdB (a Swedish company that still exists, I see). We celebrated with a Tuborg and a G and T.

The next morning we docked in Gothenburg. It was eight o'clock and still murky in the dark Swedish midwinter. The air blew starkly cold and huge lumps of ice floated in the harbour. We drove down the ramp and we were on Swedish soil. Must remember to drive on the right, we said. Signs to Göteborg (Gothenburg) and other foreign-looking places.

We soon found ourselves free of the city and rolling eastwards on a wide straight road with a hard shoulder as wide as an extra lane. An occasional tractor on the hard shoulder. It was apparent the custom was to pull over onto the hard shoulder when a faster vehicle came up behind. It was easy driving – which we shared.

We were following the green E4 signs for Stockholm – over 600km distant. We'd never seen that big a number on a signpost. Little traffic between the towns. It got to mid-morning and it was only half-light. All the traffic was still on headlights. It seemed strange to us but we realised later that that was the custom: headlights at all times. Out of the gloom in the far distance a pair of headlights would emerge, and then eventually the car or truck that they belonged to.

The countryside was flattish, and the pine forests seemed endless. The road sometimes passed through cuttings hewn out of solid black rock, sometimes covered in thick creamy foaming icicles like an overflowing pavlova. It felt like being in a Norse saga. There were surely trolls lurking in those dark pine forests. There was no snow on the ground yet; we learned later that when the snow comes, usually before January, it normally stays on the ground till spring, and everything is so much brighter, especially if it's a cold crisp sunny day.

Every now and again we'd see a battered sign by the side of the road consisting of just a capital H. Strange. It must mean something to someone, I thought. Later we learned that it was an H for *Höger* (right), reminding drivers to drive on the right: Sweden had changed to driving on the right only four years previously. Most of the signs had been removed but some in remote spots seemed to have been forgotten. The changeover must have been a daunting exercise – but not something you'd want to phase in gradually?

At one point we stopped at the side of the road to take a look around at our unfamiliar surroundings. As we opened the car door – wow! – the air hit us full in the face. It was cold and raw and exhilarating. We filled our lungs. You get insulated from the outside world being in that fuggy little box.

We had arranged to meet an SPL colleague on Sunday morning on the outskirts of Stockholm. Now as Saturday afternoon drew on, we thought we would see how far we got, and then find a small hotel for the night. The hours ticked easily away, as did the kilometres to Stockholm on the green and white boards.

Before we knew it we were in Södertälje, only 40km from Stockholm, as darkness fell about four o'clock. We came across a cosy looking hotel in the suburbs, and checked in for the night. It was comfortable, colourful and very Swedish. The biggest surprise was when I went to get two drinks from the bar. First of all, the bar was tucked away in a corner, not at all well advertised. Then, after I'd ordered a wine and a beer, the barman says, 'That will be 20 crowns' – 30 shillings in UK money. At home it would have cost 6 shillings. (At first I wrote that it cost £1.50 but that didn't quite convey the huge expense it seemed at the time. For the benefit of younger readers, £1 used to be 20 shillings). Is this a rip-off? I wondered. But no, the price of alcohol was something we soon got used to.

The following morning dawned bright and clear, and we set off in high anticipation on the last leg, to the big city, Stockholm. After a few seconds, we suddenly realised something was very wrong – I was driving on the left. I obviously needed my own internal H. Luckily there were no consequences: there was no other traffic around early on a Sunday morning.

We had arranged our rendezvous on Sunday morning at IKEA Kungens Kurva, on the outskirts of Stockholm. IKEA, what was that? It turned out to be a large furniture store, in a large circular building, five storeys high. We'd never seen such a huge furniture store. We were to get to know that building better in the months and years ahead.

When we got to IKEA we were to ring our SPL colleague John, who lived nearby, and it wasn't long before he arrived. We had a quick greeting, and he handed us each a plain white envelope with our name on it.

'Some expenses to keep you going', he said. We each opened our envelope. Each contained a number of crisp Swedish banknotes of varying colour and denomination, together with a hand-written note of explanation: a month's per diem, with deduction for the rent of our flat.

A bystander might have thought it suspicious, but it was nothing under the counter. It was just that we didn't yet have a Swedish bank account. It was a welcome and unaccustomed sight, all those new banknotes. It was reassuring to know that our employer had thought about such practical matters – even though we hadn't done any work yet. With money in our pockets and coffee in our bodies, we felt able to face whatever the world threw our way, and well-equipped to install ourselves in our new home.

2

Faraway places: Farsta and Hägersten

John led the way to our apartment. It was in Farsta ('Farshta'), a new suburb in the south-east of Stockholm. The population of Stockholm was only one million, small as European capitals go. Farsta was on the fringe of the city then, yet only 20km from the city centre. The journey took half an hour, through the outer southern suburbs. We were careful not to lose sight of our guide: no GPS or mobile phones in those days – it makes you wonder how anyone ever found their way in a strange city.

When we got to the apartment on Kristinehamnsgatan, we thanked John for his time and company, and the world was ours again. It was a typical group of apartment blocks, only three high, looking less than ten years old. Grassed areas and play equipment between the blocks. A parking

Entrance to our Farsta apartment

area well away from the play areas. The apartment itself was decorated in a pleasant modern style. The furniture was fine, no doubt from IKEA.

But – we soon realised we were lacking one thing: there was no house linen – no duvets or sheets or towels. Probably to be expected, but we hadn't. So, what to do, on a Sunday afternoon, with all the local shops closed? SPL had provided us with a ring binder full of useful facts about our new country. It told us that the department stores in the city centre were open on Sundays till 6 pm. It mentioned one store in particular that sold most things – Åhléns ('Awe-lanes'). Well, that would be an adventure on a Sunday winter afternoon.

There was an underground station at Farsta Centrum, a short walk away, so off we went to find that. This was our first experience of the Tunnelbana or T-bana (subway). We were able to buy tickets with cash – they still used cash in Sweden then. Our first ride of many on that line. The stations we passed through looked imposing, with many of them carved out of solid rock, and attractively decorated with tiles of a modern design. Each station has its own theme, so it's like moving through a huge subterranean art gallery.

After half an hour we arrived at T-centralen, the central station of the public transport system. Here were shops in underground arcades, and lots of concrete and glass. We immediately felt that this was a wonderful city to be in, and we were excited to think we would be here for a whole year at least – a long time when you're young. We revelled in the strangeness of the lettering on shop fronts and hoardings – all those letters with circles and dots on the top – how exotic was that. It was never a problem having no Swedish: in those early days we could always get by in English. But we definitely didn't want things to stay like that – we were both eager to learn the language as quickly as possible – word by word, day by day.

We soon found our way to Åhléns, then as now an iconic department store chain. Every large town and city has one. We were fascinated to see what type of products they sold – many things, big and small, took our eye. The range of soft furnishings was wide and impressive; we were spoilt for choice. But choose we did; mission accomplished. Soon we were installed in our new home, and with all our immediate needs satisfied – not bad for day one.

Another thing that we didn't have in the flat was a washing machine. However we soon realised that there was a laundry in the basement – as is the case in every Swedish apartment block. There were several washing machines and driers, and you could book a time for them. What a sensible arrangement that is.

What was also communal was the central heating – it really was central. One installation heated all the apartments; so nobody went cold. You paid a fixed amount as part of your apartment monthly rent. It would have been powered by hydroelectricity. (Nowadays often by geothermal energy – energy stored in the Earth's crust. The internet also is often communal and part of your rental contract.)

One of the unusual features of our apartment was the phone: it was like no other phone we'd ever seen before. We later learned it was common in Sweden; it was made by Ericsson and it was called, logically enough, an Ericophone. It was in one piece with a vertical handset and a circular base. No visible dial: that was under the base. And yes it was a dial: push buttons on phones hadn't been invented yet. The thing you had to remember was not to put it down upright in the middle of a conversation: that hung up the call.

We soon got to know the local area where we lived, and the walk to the shops and the T-bana. At the back of the apartment was a sports field, which had goalposts at either end, and, as well as being used for football, it was also used at other times for various sports. One day soon after we had moved in, two huge water tankers drew up and started pumping water on to the field. Strange, why does the pitch need watering in winter? For hours, days the water kept flowing. We finally realised that it had become an instant ice rink. The water froze immediately, and it stayed frozen for months. Very soon there were skaters outside our window. Did we have a go? No I didn't, I'm always wary of ice and have no balance at all. My feet would have gone from under me with relentless regularity. But we did try skiing – read on.

It became apparent that our SPL colleagues were living much nearer work, often only a five-minute drive away. That sounded like a good arrangement, so I rang the SPL office and asked if we could move to a flat nearer to work. But I was told that there were no flats available at the moment. We weren't too bothered as we weren't unhappy where we were.

There were few Minis on the road, although they had a certain cachet amongst the young. The Mini was known colloquially as a *hundkoj* (dog kennel). Cars needed special treatment in the Scandinavian winter, as well as the normal anti-freeze in the radiator that we were used to in England. You had to put *T-sprit* in the windscreen washer bottle to stop the water freezing, and *K-sprit* in the petrol tank every time you filled up to stop the petrol freezing. (Why didn't they put that in the petrol at the refinery? I wonder now. Maybe they did.) You also needed thinner oil in the engine: 10W-30 instead of the 20W-50 which was normal back home.

Hägersten apartment (the block across from us)

The temperature was often a few degrees below 0C even during the day; at night it could get down to -20C. Strange things happen in such temperatures: the snot in your nose freezes and crackles – that's a weird feeling. Apparently you need a special type of facial moisturiser that doesn't crack when frozen. But I didn't have any personal experience of that.

After four months or so, I got a call from someone in SPL personnel: 'We have an apartment available near your work.' I said I'd ring her back. Well, we ummed and ahed,

Wendy in our Hägersten apartment

do we move, or are we settled here? I called her back: 'We are happy here now, thank you.' 'No,' she says, 'we'd *like* you to move.'

So, fine, we moved – to a suburb called Hägersten ('Hay-ger-shtén'). The street was called Gösta Ekmans väg, named after the well-known Swedish actor. Everything still fitted in the car, so only one trip required. It turned out to be a good move – a more modern apartment, bigger, five floors up (of six), much nearer work. The rent was the same – a fixed amount came out of our expenses.

There were another SPL couple living in the same block, Tony and Pat. They had a two-year-old daughter. We got to know them and they asked us to baby-sit sometimes.

We were very happy to do that: their child slept all evening, and we could play their records – these were the days of vinyl. Whenever we hear George Harrison and *My Sweet Lord*, it takes us back to that time and place. (We hadn't got the *All Things Must Pass* LP.) When we were back in Sweden some months later, jobless and homeless, Tony and Pat bought us a slap-up meal in a restaurant. We were grateful to them.

The evenings were long and light. When we weren't out enjoying the outdoors, we used to enjoy being at home listening to our own music, either on our own or with friends. Another record that takes us back is *Let It Be*, which had just been released. In particular Paul singing *The Long And Winding Road*.

A young woman lived in a ground floor apartment. She was good-looking in a Swedish way, slim with long blonde hair. We walked past her door on the way to the lift. Often she would be greeting a male visitor, or saying goodbye to one. The funny thing was, it was always a different man. She's got a lot of friends, I thought.

There was a car park in the basement of the block, with a steepish ramp down to it. On weekday mornings the snow had already been cleared by the time we left. One Saturday morning however we drove out expecting to sail up the ramp as usual; we only got a metre or two before the wheels were spinning madly and we were getting nowhere. Clearly snow-clearing did not have the same priority at the weekend. Within an hour or two the snow had been cleared and we could escape.

3

LM Ericsson

Back to Farsta briefly – from our first flat it was a twenty-five minute drive to work. The office was in an inner suburb so we didn't have to drive into the centre of Stockholm. The route to work quickly became automatic, as it does. Often it had been snowing overnight, and the snow lay thick on the car in the cold crisp morning. We scraped the ice off inside and out. And, remarkably, the car started every day. Work began at eight, so it was still dark when we left home. In midwinter the sun doesn't rise till nine and it sets at three, and during those few daylight hours it's often only half-light, especially if it's cloudy or drizzly. The roads had always been cleared of snow – they clearly had that down to a fine art. With the heater on full bore, and trying to keep the windscreen from icing up, we followed the line of cars in front at a steady pace through the gloom. At least there were never any major hold-ups.

We found our way to the office at Telefonplan (Telephone Square). There was ample parking there. Each parking space had an electrical outlet on a post so you could plug your Volvo or Saab in, so that it wasn't totally frozen when it was time to go home. No such facility on a humble Mini sadly.

LM Ericsson were (and still are) a major employer in Stockholm and a large international corporation. They made almost every telephone handset in Sweden, and many in international markets also. The project we were working on was developing the software for a public telephone exchange. This was a major IT application at that time – previously public phone exchanges had been electro-mechanical (analogue).

The product that we were working on was called AKE (*Automatiska Kodväljarbaserade Elektronikväxlar* or Computer Controlled Exchanges). LM Ericsson were one of the players competing in an international industry along with a handful of global hi-tech companies. Development of the product required a massive financial investment – on our project there were fifty software engineers, and a similar number of hardware engineers. The timescale of the project was measured in years, in the order of five to ten years. This investment was justified by the huge potential rewards of supplying exchanges to telephone administrations all round the world.

In 1971 the state of Information Technology was primitive compared to today. This was long before the personal computer was invented. There were only mainframes, large and weighty, costing upwards of hundreds of thousands of dollars, in air-conditioned rooms with false floors. All the cabling ran under the false floors. A PC today would be more powerful than some of the mainframes then.

I have to say that I was never excited by my work – either in this job or in any other. But at least this was a hands-on programming project and the work turned out to be quite interesting, although I'd never worked on telephone switching systems before. You didn't have to understand the whole concept, just the bit you were working on. The programming language was what was known as a low-level assembler. As opposed to a high-level language, in assembler all instructions are broken down into basic arithmetic and logical operations. It took a long time (weeks, months) to code an application. Within a few years, assembler language would no longer be used for application software. Assembler language had the advantage of being fast to run as it was close to the computer's native language.

For some unknown reason I kept a few pages of one of my programs, and a sample of it appears here. I probably wanted to keep some evidence that I had actually produced something to justify all the money they were paying me. The program doesn't make any sense to me now. That incidentally is one of the drawbacks of a low level language:

```
Mdf

6JUL71 RUN ON TAPE:   LNE/APZ130/*/KH/NC/348/4JUL71                        PAGE   17
     0               PROGRAM      CILL/2/3ALARM/GSH/6JUL71
     1     ! TASK PROGRAM CONTAINING COMMAND ROUTINES TO:
     2     ! 1. STEP DOWN INDICATED ALARM COUNTER
     3     ! 2. PRINT DETAILS OF 32 LATEST ALARMS VIA MESSAGES FROM BOTH BUFFERS
     4     ! 3. TEST ALARM CIRCUITS AND LAMPS
     5     ! 4. INHIBIT ALARM TEST
     6                CUE          ****
     7    SDAL:       CONALAC      TO CODE                             ! D:C0*ALARM CODE
     8                LCH          A%=D
     9                LBU          A,7                                 ! TO STEP SPRUNCB COUNTER
    10                STALARM
    11    EXEC:       COMEND
    12    NOTACC:     COMEND       NOT ACC
    13                CUE          ****
    14    TALA:       LAS          M=M*C!MD(25)
    15                LHS          DM=IB*2                             ! TALACTR
    16                CCC          A=1,R                               ! IS NEXT CHAR DOT
    17                JUMP         TALAINH
    18                ACHM         D=1
    19                JCU          NOTACC                              ! IF TALACTR=255
    20                LOVA         A**10                               ! SET A!C1=1
    21                JUMP         COMM
    22    ! INHIBIT PART
    23    TALAINH:    LWM          A=IC(1)
    24    ! TEST ON LETTERS IN
    25                JUMPIF       A**#EK9 TO NOTACC
    26                NEXPA
    27                CCU          A=1,R
    28                JUMP         NOTACC                              ! IF NEXT CHAR NOT DOT
    29                TRL          D=D,7                               ! IS TALACTR 0
    30                JUMP         NOTACC                              ! YES
    31                DCSH         IB,2=1                              ! NO, DECREMENT IT
    32                LOVA         A*0                                 ! SET A!C1=0
    33    COMM:       LCC          A!0=C!ANUM
    34    STEP:       STALARM
    35                DCHC         A=1
    36                JCE          STEP                                ! JUMP IF ALARM CODE GE 0
    37    STOP:       TRH          A,4,R                               ! WAS THIS AN INHIBIT
```

Code fragment

the meaning is not immediately obvious just from looking at the code – you needed to write textual documentation to explain to your successors what the program was doing. Some programmers were better than others in that regard. It seems that I wasn't among the better ones.

We wrote our programs on squared-paper coding sheets, which were then punched onto computer-readable cards – we never got to see that part of the process. Then the cards were read in by the mainframe, which was also in some unknown room somewhere, and a day or two later the output was returned to the programmer. A world away from how things happen today when every developer has a screen and you can run and test your work instantaneously.

LM Ericsson

There were twenty or so programmers on contract from SPL. Apparently there were not enough experienced Swedish programmers. It certainly wasn't the case that we were cheaper. In fact, after SPL had loaded up our daily rate many times, we would have been hugely expensive.

The offices were modern and made for a good working environment – as you would expect at a company like Ericsson. Each office was occupied by two or three people. I shared an office with an SPL colleague Paul and an American guy Jack; there were a team of Americans also on the project, from Columbus, Ohio. Wendy shared an office with Bill, another American.

There were some interesting communication issues at times: two countries divided by a common language. A lot of the US words were familiar from American movies. Sometimes not. Once I was giving directions to Jack and said, 'Go straight on at the roundabout.' Blank look. Eventually we got to, 'Oh you mean a circle.' Another time we gave Jack a lift – he looked at the Mini in disbelief: 'This is a *car*?!' He was even more dumbfounded when he couldn't find the rear door (it didn't have one – Minis only had two doors back then). Not to mention the steering wheel being on the wrong side.

Jack was also surprised at Swedish cultural norms. One evening on TV there was a scene with a naked woman. The next day he couldn't believe it: 'you could see *everything*!' (Not much has changed in that regard: even today a naked breast on US TV seems to be taboo.) Which reminds me of another exchange between Jack and me: once he was talking about a 'bre-zear'. I couldn't work out what on earth he meant. Pardon, I said a few times. He was getting redder and redder. Eventually I got it. 'Oh you mean a bra.' Sorry Jack. I can't remember why we were talking about that.

Our immediate manager was Skugge, a smart (intelligent) and friendly person. He called himself just by his surname, as did most of the managers. He wore wooden clogs (*träskor*) to the office. His English was faultless. It was so good that in a meeting held in Swedish, he would sit in the row behind and, leaning forward, translate *sotto voce* sentence by sentence: translating one sentence while listening to the next. You've got to be good to do that. All the technical documentation was in English, as were all our technical meetings, but we were picking up Swedish day by day just by being there. For us, that was part of the thrill of being in a foreign country.

We were well looked after by SPL. Our Ericsson ID card was over-stamped 'Fri Lunch'. I wondered what was special about lunch on Fridays. Nothing, it turned out – it meant Free Lunch. Another perk of the job. There was a huge canteen downstairs which catered for all the many hundreds of workers. Our ID cards did indeed let us have a free lunch. It was a good introduction to everyday Swedish food – mostly very acceptable and healthy and familiar. There was also the 'Grill'. You had to pay a bit extra to eat from the Grill, but they had more exciting things like grilled food (surprise) and even chips. Sometimes we indulged.

Wendy at beach picnic

Another popular Swedish custom we were introduced to was *fika* (coffee and cake) which is an essential part of mid-mornings. On a Friday, somebody from a different section would come and give us a talk about what they were working on, while we listened and enjoyed the coffee and cake.

A common practice in Sweden was that workplaces had shorter hours in summer. Most of the year we worked eight till five with an hour for lunch. But in June, July and August we finished at four. It's said that *sommar* is one of hardest Swedish words to translate. To a Swede it means so much more than just summer: it means light, it means warmth, it means being outside, it means holidays. More about summer, and Midsummer in particular, later.

SPL hosted a number of social events for employees and partners. On one occasion there was a picnic on an island in the archipelago. Nobody went in to the water – it was still icy cold.

Our contract was initially from January until August – although we were never told that. Strange that it never occurred to us to ask. When August came, some of our colleagues were taken off the project and went back to the UK, but Wendy and I were told that our contracts had been extended till the end of the year, so we must have been doing something right. We were very happy about that – we were having a great time.

In December there was a Christmas dinner at a local restaurant for all the people in our workgroup. LM paid for it all, including food, drinks and entertainment. It was very well organised: somebody had put together a whole wadge of papers containing an invitation, the menu, song lyrics, jokes, even a flowchart of how the evening was to proceed. Each of us got our own copy. I still have mine. (Does this make me a hoarder?) The invitation page appears here. I get some of the jokes, which display a keen sense of humour – something which had not been evident to me at the time. Most of the jokes are beyond me – Swedish wordplay, in-jokes etc. Here's one I did get:

A jobseeker comes to the HR department at LM. The HR manager asks him where he's been earlier.

Invitation to office party

– I've been at Volvo, Saab and IBM
– What were you doing there?
– Looking for a job.

So much for the working day. Let's go back to the beginning and have some fun.

4

Helena

Helena ('He-lé-na') gets a chapter to herself. She deserves it.

We both looked forward to the weekends when we could explore our new home. One place we soon discovered was the Tudor Arms, a British pub in Östermalm, an older district in the centre of Stockholm. British as in beer and food and staff and interior, even a dartboard. What wasn't so familiar were the prices. They had some good English beers on tap, but a pint cost 6.5 kronor. A pound sterling was 12.5 kr. So a pint cost about ten shillings, whereas we were used to two shillings a pint back home. A bit of a shock at first, but you got used to it.

Helena, Mia, Wendy

We often used to visit on Saturday lunchtimes, have a pint or two and a bite to eat. We would often bump into our work colleagues. One day Vic was there with his girlfriend Helena. We were immediately drawn to Helena. Not just because she was a lively girl, about twenty years old, and sounding very English. She worked for the Anglo-Swedish Chamber of Commerce. She talked about her time living in Battersea in London. She had a bit of a Battersea accent ('Ba'sea') – yes, a London girl for sure. We soon got to know Helena well, as we were often in the Tudor Arms together, or at various parties. We were often round at her flat in Gärdet, an inner city suburb, and she introduced us to her friends Kennet and Mia. One day I heard her speaking fluent Swedish with Mia.

Two roses in the spring sunshine

'How come you speak such good Swedish?', I asked her. 'I *am* Swedish', she replied.

Well fancy that, you had me there. Helena's English was (is) so good she could have been a spy. She even had the everyday expressions: 'Let's get cracking!' was a favourite, or 'I haven't seen her in donkey's years'. The only time I heard her slip up was when she asked for a faggy. Luckily I knew what she meant. 'You can call it a ciggy or a fag but not a faggy.'

Helena became our guide to Sweden and all things Swedish. We met her mother, her brother, and her sister and family. Helena generously included us in her Midsummer family celebrations, and also on Christmas Eve. She taught us how to *skål* when drinking aquavit (snaps), and a number of accompanying songs. The rules are simple: take your full snaps glass, raise it to your third button, sing the agreed song, look everyone in the eye in turn, say *'skål'*, down the glass in one, repeat the eye contact routine, glass back on the table. Note: no clinking of glasses.

And fifty years later, we are still good friends with Helena, and see her whenever we're in Sweden. She later joined the Swedish Foreign Office and spent many years in Swedish Embassies round the world, including Cairo and Lima. Helena later became head of a Swedish Child Protection Non-Government Organisation. A good person and a strong woman and very Swedish. The Queen of Sweden was the patron of the NGO, and Helena came to be on good terms with the Queen. Once, more recently, when Helena was in the supermarket queue, the Queen rang: 'Good morning Your Majesty…'.

Another character we met in the Tudor Arms was Arne ('Áre-ne'). It must have been about February 1971 that we first met him.

Arne was a lot older than us, at least thirty, maybe even late thirties. He used to be a taxi driver in Copenhagen, and now did the same in Stockholm. He was a bulky sort of man, and looked as though he enjoyed a beer or two. He had a strong Danish accent. He never told us why he left Denmark, and you wouldn't want to ask. He was a bit of a lovable rogue, a rough diamond. Arne had some favourite English sayings: 'I take a beeer' (yes, first impressions were correct) and 'not a fair chaaance'. He was always on the lookout for a deal. For some reason he seemed to like being with English people. We hadn't known Arne long when I mentioned that I was thinking of buying an SLR camera. His ears pricked up.

'I get you a real nice camera, just leave it to me.'

A few days later he turns up at our flat with a brand new Minolta SRT-101 complete with box and glossy instruction book with examples of the kind of arty photos that I dreamt of taking. A top of the range SLR. Something that would have been beyond my wildest dreams a few months previously.

'I had one stolen, and the insurance gave me this one.' I didn't pursue it. I picked the camera up, and immediately fell in love with it. Arne as usual had a fag hanging out of his mouth, and was blowing smoke and ash all over this beautiful thing. It would have cost £100 or more in the UK – 1250 kronor.

'I tell you what I do. I can let you have it for 600. And we can do it this way (another favourite Arne-ism). You don't pay me now, just give me a cheque for 625 with the date at the end of the month. And don't write who the cheque is for.'

So that's what I did. I suppose he had a mate at the taxi rank who cashed cheques. Arne got the 600 now, and his mate banked the cheque at the end of the month. Good thing the cheque didn't bounce – it could have got nasty for me. Why didn't I just give him 600 cash, I'm wondering now. It would have been simpler (and cheaper).

Arne said he'd give me a receipt. That would be useful going back through UK customs: they were always on the look-out for expensive items obtained abroad, and you could get slapped with hefty import duty. The receipt turned out to be from a small pad that you could buy at any newsagent, on cheap paper, with no company logo, handwritten and for the 600 I'd paid. But at least it did have a serial number. The only problem was it was 000001.

The next time I went back to the UK, I did indeed get stopped at customs. He asked me if I had a 'receipt for the camera, Sir?' I showed him my pathetic piece of paper. He tried hard not to laugh, but there was the flicker of a smile. All he said was, 'You certainly got a good deal there, Sir'. I agreed. But he didn't charge me any duty.

It turned out to be a great camera. I took mostly slides, and experimented a bit with black and white film. I still have hundreds of slides in boxes, which need to be culled severely and the better ones scanned into digital. The photo on the front cover was taken with this camera. The first picture ever taken with it is the one of us two on the back cover. Yes I know it's out of focus: it's a deliberate decision to get a softer look. Or you could say it's a crack to let the light in.

5

A week in Czechoslovakia

Very soon after we met Arne he started talking about a trip to Prague. He'd been there a few times and he loved it there, partly because of the low price of everything, especially the beer (*pivo*). He also liked the lack of rules and regulations there, unlike in Sweden. In 1968 – only three years previously – Czechoslovakia had seen the Prague Spring: months of mass protest and political liberalisation when their leader Dubcek had brought in several reforms. That is, until the Russians said '*Nyet*' and invaded in August 1968. Now in 1971 the Russian Army was still in charge; tourism was practically non-existent. But were we deterred? – no we were not.

On the contrary we didn't need any convincing that a week's trip to Prague would be very exciting. It would be Arne, Helena and us two (Arne was no doubt hoping to get

East German visa with entry and exit dates

to know Helena better). Behind the Iron Curtain, as it then was. A world we'd only ever read about in the papers, or seen on TV. (Also a world away from the Prague of today. See page 54.) The plan was to drive down in Arne's Rover 2000, via Denmark and East Germany. Six nights in Prague, then back via Poland and East Germany.

A week in Czechoslovakia

We had to get visas for East Germany, Czechoslovakia and Poland, so we entrusted our passports to Arne, so that he could get visas from the relevant embassies in Stockholm. I suspect there were no queues: only a few crazy foreigners like us.

By April 4th already we were on our way. Things happen fast when you're young. A 600km drive down to Malmö in the south-west of Sweden, ferry to Copenhagen – long before the Öresund bridge had even been dreamed of – then another 150km down to Gedser on the south coast of Denmark. It was mostly trucks and truck drivers on the ferry: Eastern Europeans were not allowed to travel to the West. And there were few Danes or Swedes who wanted to go to the grey communist East, especially in winter. Maybe a few who bought a few crates of duty-free beer, and got the ferry straight back: that would explain the empty trolley some men had with them. It was only a two-hour trip on the ferry, we took a beeer (in Arne-speak), and we got to Warnemünde late in the evening.

We were the only foreign car off the ferry that night. Our first experience of Eastern Europe was the strict Communist security – out of the car, passports and visas closely inspected. (But not as thorough as when we left the Eastern bloc – then they were looking for hidden human cargo – more of that later.) We were escorted into the office where we had to buy a certain amount of East German Marks, so much for each day we were there: the East German government wanted hard western currency.

And at the official rate of exchange – which was a poor rate compared to what you could get on the street – also more of which later.

Officially an East German Mark was equal to one West German Mark – the Deutschmark – whereas on the street you could get 5 eastern marks for 1 DM – but that was illegal. As we were soon to discover, all our expenses such as hotels and petrol and food were cheap, even at the official rate. And we didn't see anything that we wanted to take home with us – apart from classic Bohemian glassware. There were a lot of things which were taken for granted in the west – jeans and perfume and western music for example – which were unobtainable in the East. There were stories of such things being smuggled into the East.

Then they asked Arne for his Green Card – the international car insurance document. Surprisingly Arne had one. The guard studies it closely then as he hands it back, he points to something on the form. Oh no, surely not a problem? But the guard only says, 'write name here!' Arne had used it many times before and never signed it. Then they wave us through. Phew, we got through without any hassle. As Arne drives off, he says, 'Dummkopf! He didn't even notice that it was three years out of date!' And so it was. That was Arne. Later he showed us a hidden slot under the dashboard where he had US$50 in $1 bills (a lot of money). 'Just in case', he says. Just in case he needed to keep somebody sweet, I supposed.

A week in Czechoslovakia

East Germany really was a totalitarian state in those days. At the border they'd given us a map of the allowed transit routes. These were the only roads on which foreigners were allowed to travel. And there were very few of them – maybe only a dozen in the whole country – only one for example went to the Czech border at Zinnwald. That was via Rostock, Neubrandenburg, Prenzlau and Dresden, a distance of over 500km. There were also only a very limited number of petrol stations where you were allowed to fill up, which were also marked on the map.

There was little traffic around at this time of night. Arne remembered the route from previous trips. In any case he wouldn't have wanted to be seen using a map. By the time we'd got past Rostock and its huge grey blocks of flats, it was past midnight. Even though it was an official transit route, it was only a single lane road winding through the sleeping villages. Arne pulls off into a layby. 'We better get some sleeep' he says. Any of us would have been happy to drive, but Arne didn't suggest it. The car was full of cigarette smoke as we were all smokers – some more than others. That's how it was in those days. We tried to sleep but no-one did. After a few minutes, Arne says 'Aaaach we keep going'. And we drove on through the night.

Just after Prenzlau, we joined the autobahn which took us south to the outskirts of Berlin. The road was one of Hitler's infamous motorways which had been built in the 1930s. It was built of concrete and was straight and fast but they hadn't joined the sections very well, so every few seconds you'd get a bump as you went over a join. That gets to be wearing after a few hours. There was little traffic still – mostly grey Russian Army trucks and tanks on the back of low-loaders. Scary stuff.

We stopped at a service station in the middle of nowhere and filled up. All the local traffic ran on very low octane fuel – it was only at the designated petrol stations where you could get premium fuel. The building was drab and functional and colourless. We bought some food with our funny-looking money. Dawn broke and found us driving through the middle of Dresden, a city infamous for its heavy bombardment during the war. There were no signs of that, which was something, but the overall impression was one of greyness and dilapidation. A light drizzle was falling and we drove past bus stops where the people waiting looked resigned and hopeless. Maybe it was just the weather they were resigned to. Or maybe it's the same the world over early on a wet Monday morning in winter.

Only 50km now to the Czech border. The road was again single lane, and the signs pointed to Zinnwald, the German town on the border, not to a town or city in Czechoslovakia. We get to the East German border control and the security is even tighter than when entering the country. Now they're looking for people trying to smuggle themselves out of the country. So it's the flexible stick into the petrol tank to check that it really is a petrol tank and not a human hiding place. And the mirror on a trolley jack underneath the car to check

En route to Prague: Graham, Helena, Arne, Wendy

for a person under the car – how would that work? But no person was found hidden in or under the car and we were allowed to pass – a few hundred metres further on we reached the Czech border control.

Again the changing of hard currency into Czech korunas, so much per day that we would be there. But the Czech guards were not quite as stony-faced as the East Germans – and, unlike in Germany, nobody expects you to have a word of Czech, so English is the normal language in these situations. We were soon on our way again. Arne was happy to be in his beloved Czechoslovakia. Only 100km more to Praha (Prague) through flat farmland and sparse traffic.

Before we got to Prague, it was time for a break and refreshment; it was about midday, the rain had stopped and the sun had appeared. We stopped at a small cafe/restaurant along the way. Old building, tables and chairs out the front, no one around. All out in the fields no doubt. A friendly chap comes to take the order – 'Four *pivo*!' says Arne with a big smile on his face. Arne's main reason for coming all this way (apart from getting to know Helena better) was to get stuck into the local beer. 'Just a minute', we say 'not all of us drink beer'. So then it was three *pivo* and something else, not sure what, all these years later. The beer was worth the long trip and we tucked into a hearty goulash.

As was to be the case generally, it was a satisfying meal and tasty, even if there wasn't much variety. If it wasn't goulash, it was steak – which meant a good size piece of meat, reasonably tender, boiled potatoes, some gravy and the final flourish – a fried egg on top of the steak. We drank the coffee a few times – where available – and it was always the same – tiny cups, strong coffee with the bottom half of the cup being sludgy coffee – Turkish style. Probably a luxury locally, and it satisfied our need for caffeine. But it was much safer to stick to the beer, which was delicious – and cheap. The whole meal wouldn't have cost more than a few dollars.

Before long we were in the centre of Prague. Russian tanks and soldiers were everywhere, but nobody seemed to take any notice of them. We had no hotel booked of course.

Wendy and Helena (or is it Agnetha and Anni-Frid?)

We parked up and went into a hotel – quite grand and ornate and old – and asked if they had any rooms free. We wanted three rooms – one for Arne, one for Helena and one for us. 'No rooms', says the man behind the desk. Strange, considering there was hardly a tourist to be seen, apart from us. Maybe it was full of Russian army officers. Looking back, I'm surprised Arne didn't slip a few US dollars under the counter. Possibly what the man was waiting for. Or it could simply have been that hotels were not allowed to take foreigners.

We tried a few more city hotels – always 'no rooms'. So we thought oh well – let's head out from Prague into the country. We eventually came across a small town with

Wendy in Wenceslas Square, Prague

a nice looking hotel near the middle of town. And they had three rooms available. They maybe hadn't been told about the 'no foreigners' rule. We booked in for three nights. Again, it was old – but clean and comfortable. As were the beds. The buffet breakfast was also a treat.

The next day we headed back to Prague to check out the city. Arne knew the city well, and had his favourite haunts. He found a cafe in Wenceslas Square – a name that had been much in the news since the invasion. A Russian tank still brooded in the middle of the square, threatening. But the streets were busy; people going about their everyday lives. We sat down and ordered. 'Four *pivo!*' says Arne. 'No, Arne...'.

Helena and early model Skoda

There was a Russian soldier at a nearby table. Arne had a carrier bag with him and he delves into it and takes out a large can of Carlsberg. He goes over to the soldier and they're having a bit of a laugh together, and Arne gives him the can of Carlsberg. The soldier looks very happy, puts it in his pocket and duly wanders off, smiling. A few minutes later, he's back, not smiling now. And he gives Arne the can of beer back. 'Forbidden', he says, in accented English, and makes a hasty retreat. An officer must have seen it, given him a mouthful about taking gifts from foreigners and told him to take it back.

As mentioned, the official exchange rate for the Czech Koruna (crown) was very low – so you got not many crowns for your western currency. You could get a much better rate on the street. The only problem was it was highly illegal to exchange at other than the official rate. The penalty was severe – confiscation of your money or maybe even time behind bars. This didn't deter Arne. His tried and trusted method of doing a deal was to walk around wearing an almost transparent nylon white shirt with a wad of US greenbacks showing in his breast pocket. And he did do a deal or two – without getting caught or mugged down a dark alley.

> *We went back to Prague in 2017 for the first time since that visit in 1971. We wanted to know what it would be like 46 years later. Well, as you may imagine, totally unrecognisable in some respects. We walked round Wenceslas Square – with many many other tourists (yes we were part of the problem) but the good thing about it was that the previously faded grandeur of the buildings had been lovingly restored. Along with freedom. And the tourist trade. The beer, and the food, were still excellent.*

In the evening we went to a nightclub with plush seating and a small stage. We ate our favourite meal – steak with a fried egg on top. Together with a few beers – and of course a something else. Then the lights went down and they had a bit of a floor show. But there was not much atmosphere as there were not many people in for the show – no doubt way over budget for the average citizen.

It was well into the evening by the time we headed back to our hotel. It was an hour's drive or so, but Arne was happy to drive. 'I've only had a couple of beeeers', he said. We finally got to our little hotel in the country. It must have been about 11pm, no later. But to our dismay the front door was locked. Nobody had said anything about closing time; there was probably a sign on the door in Czech. Now late at night, there were no lights inside, nobody to be seen. Oh dear! we said to ourselves. We pulled at the door a few times, but it didn't want to open. Our efforts were making a lot noise in the silent sleeping town, and dogs began to bark.

Then Arne says 'I feeex it' – and he gives it an almighty Danish shoulder. The door bursts open with a loud bang, luckily with no broken glass. The door was old enough that there was a bit of play somewhere. We all run up the grand wide staircase and luckily we have our room keys with us, and we two arrive breathlessly in our darkened room. Then, no more than ten minutes later, we hear cars driving up and parking right outside just below our room. Then raised voices in the hotel. We held our breath and pretended to be asleep.

We waited for a bang on the door. But surely they couldn't know it was us – or could they? What would they do to us – sling us in jail probably for breaking and entering. But knock came there none, and eventually the cars drove away, no doubt scratching their heads and wondering who on earth had broken in in the middle of the night – and disappeared. And why, what had they been after? I could imagine the police turning over the local usual suspects and them protesting 'it wasn't me guv honest.'

The next morning at breakfast we half expected a bit of an inquest, but things were just the same as usual.

After our three days near Prague, we decided to drive down to Bratislava for two nights. Prague was in the north of the country – what is now Czechia/Czech Republic – whereas Bratislava is in the south – now Slovakia – and was the second city of Czechoslovakia. It was a distance of 330km, via Brno.

It was exciting to be on the open road again, travelling yet further east, more east than we'd ever been before. One of the main roads of the country, yet little traffic. Time to stop for a bite to eat. A roadside inn. We sit down at a table and check the menu, in German as well as Czech. Wurst was on offer, and a wide selection of *pivo*.

'Four *pivo*!' orders Arne, looking thirsty. 'No, Arne…'.

Bratislava is a mere 10km from the Austrian border, and 70km from Vienna, but it was then a world away in reality, across a heavily secured border and a lot of barbed wire.

Since the reunification of Europe you can travel between the two cities completely freely – by train, by road or by boat on the Danube – within the hour. You can't put a price on freedom.

A week in Czechoslovakia

We happened upon a large modern-looking hotel in Bratislava and had no problem booking three rooms. The coffee was of the same thick consistency, the steak with fried egg on top was the same, and the *pivo* was still excellent. We walked down through the old city centre to the Danube, which was maybe 100 metres wide, with a few commercial barges around but no pleasure craft – and definitely no cruise ships.

In the evening we fancied a bit of light relief so we thought we'd find a disco. We jumped in a taxi outside the hotel. We asked the driver to take us to a disco – that was surely an international word. He nods knowingly. After twenty minutes we seem to be going out of the city. Funny. Now we're in the countryside with green fields all around. Strange place for a disco. So – words and miming with the driver. 'Disco – music – dancing?' Something clicks. 'Ah! disco!'. And he promptly turns round and drives back the way he came. We must have been on our way to a village called Disko many miles away. It's funny looking back, but we weren't laughing then. By the time we got back to the city we were in no mood for dancing, so the taxi took us back to the hotel. The fare would have been small. We spent a quiet evening doing nothing special.

The next day was our last day in Czechoslovakia. Arne's getting a bit grumpy by now, possibly because there haven't been any developments in his relationship with Helena. 'I know a little town on the booor-der', he says, 'we go there'. It turns out to be Mlada Boleslav, near the Polish border, and 350km from Bratislava. Presumably Arne had some history in this town. We find a beautiful old hotel in the town centre and they have rooms. Nice to be in a smaller town. No getting back to the hotel late at night this time.

The next morning we head off towards the Polish border, only 80km away. The plan is to cut across the very south-western corner of Poland and enter East Germany on its eastern border. We are soon there and there's the normal close scrutiny on both sides of the border. With entry stamps added to the Polish visa in our passports, we head for Frankfurt-an-der-Oder, 250km away.

We drive through a rural landscape, with scattered farms and small villages. As in the other communist bloc countries, the overriding impression is one of greyness and a simple agricultural way of life. More tractors than cars. I got to drive the Rover 2000 for some of the way. That was fun.

The all-important *pivo* would no doubt be as good here, but we don't stop: probably because we don't pass a cafe. Within a few hours we are at the border. The border guard examines our passports, and sees that we have been all of four hours in his country. He looks up angrily. 'Too fast!' he says, the unspoken accusation being that we are treating his country as a short-cut. Which we are of course. But, shaking his head, he gives our passports a heavy stamp and waves us on.

A long high bridge over the River Oder looms up, a natural no-mans-land. We're at the East German border. Helena innocently gets out her camera for a pic of the magnificent river and bridge. 'Nein!' comes the sharp rebuke. Lucky they didn't confiscate it. We're asked where we want to go. Warnemünde, we tell him. 'That's not a transit route today', the guard says, 'you go to Berlin'. Our visas are overwritten by hand to show our new route. Berlin, that sounds exciting, we think. Berlin, a name that rings through history, even for our post-war generation. It's only two hours or so to West Berlin, where the stipulated entry point is at Drewitz, near Potsdam, where the historic 1945 conference was held with Churchill, Stalin and Truman. The outcome of that meeting and of the War itself – the Iron Curtain – is only too apparent in this part of Europe. It's strange looking back to think that those events happened only twenty-six years previously.

We only had a few hours in West Berlin but differences with the East were striking – the prosperity, the number and type of cars, the outdoor life. We visited Checkpoint Charlie, the main crossing point between West and East Berlin – you see the historic sign in English, French, German and Russian: 'You are now leaving the American sector'. We weren't crossing here but at Staaken, not that far away, in a few hours' time. How privileged we were that we had the choice to come and go.

From Staaken it was only three hours up the autobahn to the port of Warnemünde. From there the ferry back to

Gedser in Denmark. As Arne's heading north, he says, 'we take a little stop in Køge'. It's his home town and his mother still lives there. It's a short way off the main road, and we're soon in Køge. I don't know if we were expected, but it's a lovely little Danish house in a row in a quiet street, with lots of flowers in the front yard. Arne's mother is smiling and welcoming. We don't stay long, and then we're off on the long drive back to Stockholm. We'd only been away for nine days but we'd learned a lot, seen a lot and hadn't spent much money. And we had a beautiful pale blue bowl in Bohemian glass – which we still have – to prove it wasn't a dream.

6

Summer with Belle

After we got back from Prague in the middle of April, it was getting warmer in Stockholm and summer was clearly on its way. The snow had melted and everything was more colourful and brighter. What was even more noticeable was that the days were getting longer. As mentioned earlier, *sommar* is so important in Sweden. One of the biggest weekends in the Swedish calendar is Midsummer. A bit of a misnomer really because it's only Midsummer in a calendar sense: the weather can still be cool and it marks the beginning of *sommar*, which lasts only till the end of August. That's when life returns to normal – when everyone's holidays are over and the schools go back.

But now in spring there was talk among the SPL people of buying a boat for the summer. A boat?! Me? It seemed incredible that a penniless student like me a short time ago would be considering buying a boat. I was still paying off the overdraft that I'd run up while I was a student. But that was back home and the Swedish bank account was showing a credit balance.

It quickly emerged that four of us were keen on the idea – Peter, Stuart and us two. We checked out the Boats For Sale ads in *Dagens Nyheter*, one of the national newspapers. Soon we found an advert for a good-sounding boat on Lidingö, a large island to the north-east of the city centre. It was a 1948 Pettersson boat, a traditional wooden motorboat which were still being built until not long before.

So we went over one evening to have a look at her. She was on land, just to the north of Gamla Lidingöbron. All boats are taken out of the water over winter, a process know as *winteruppläggning* (winter laying-up). If you forget, your boat will be in a sorry state next spring: it will have been crushed by the melting ice.

She was just what we were looking for – a few prods of the hull suggested no rot, she would carry four to six people, and she even had a small cabin in the bow with two sleeping berths. The owner, an old chap with a weather-beaten face, explained that she started on petrol, then when the engine was warm, you could switch over to *fotogen* (paraffin), which was cheaper. The asking price was 4000 kronor (£320). £80 each. It wasn't worth haggling, and we said we'd take it. He was happy, and so were we. The boat was called Belle, displayed in brass letters on her stern. And so began our summer with Belle.

Summer with Belle

I couldn't help thinking of the Ingmar Bergman film *Sommaren med Monika*. It starred a young Harriet Andersson and told of her teenage affair with her boyfriend Harry; they borrowed a boat – a Pettersson boat just like ours – and escaped the adult world for a few weeks of passion in the beauty and light of the Stockholm *skärgården* (archipelago, literally rock garden) in summer.

Belle was seeing out the winter among several other boats in a boatyard by the edge of the water. On a certain day in May all the boats would be hoisted back into the water. We had a month or so to do any maintenance work that was required on the hull and engine.

The evenings were getting lighter so we'd come over to the boatyard after work, or at the weekend, and scrape the hull of barnacles and do other nautical things, such as painting below the waterline. The woodwork had weathered beautifully over the years, and we gave it another coat of varnish. Stuart knew of a ship chandlers just round the corner, where we availed ourselves of grommets and suchlike.

We got the engine started without too much trouble, and she ran smoothly enough – on dry land. We greased the stern gland too – it seemed the right thing to do.

The great day came when it was time for Belle to be reunited with the water. We watched like proud parents from the quayside: the operation was handled by a professional team. Before long it was Belle's turn. The crane arm was extended several metres so that it reached

Belle takes to the air

out over our boat. Two hessian straps were placed under the bow and stern. The crane took the strain and then Belle was flying through the air, and gently plopped into the water, and pulled back to shore.

Soon we were able to go aboard. The moment of truth – we turned the key in the ignition and pressed the red button – she started! Then into gear and off she moved. She seemed to be moving at a hefty lick, but no doubt out on open water it wouldn't seem so fast. She did about eight knots max. She was perfect for our needs.

The next thing we needed was a mooring. It was Peter who found a perfect spot in a boatyard at Biskopsudden, on Djurgården, a beautiful island in the centre of Stockholm. Djurgården has many historic villas, parks and museums,

Near Biskopsudden on Djurgården

including the Vasa Museum and the Skansen open-air museum.

> *In 2019 we were back on Djurgården and it was still green and peaceful, and our boatyard was still there and full of expensive boats. We also visited the wonderful Prins Eugen's Waldemarsudde art museum, something we hadn't taken the time to search out in 1971.*

The boatyard was on the south of the island, between Slussen, the large lock in the centre of Stockholm which separates the inland waters from the vast and beautiful *skärgården* which lies between Stockholm and the Baltic Sea. The *skärgården* stretches out like a giant fan from

On uninhabited island: Stuart, Gunna, Wendy, Jo, Ivor

Stockholm, consisting of some five thousand islands, mostly uninhabited and maybe only a few metres long. Some are just black granite rocks sticking out of the water. It's all of 100km before you get to the open sea; we never got anywhere near that far out. That would have taken hours – days even.

The boatyard had four pontoons, with some large expensive boats there. Even back then it was quite hard to get a mooring; I don't know how Peter found it – he must have known somebody. There was a small cafe there too, where you could buy coffee and snacks. A special treat we sometimes allowed ourselves was a *smörgås med räkor* – an open shrimp sandwich with mayonnaise and

Log for 5th June is for the campfire trip

hard-boiled egg and a sprig of dill. It tasted as delicious as it sounds.

We bought a large-scale chart of the inner archipelago, with depths marked – an essential item to have on board in this rocky world. In the summer months – June, July and August – the working day finished an hour earlier, at four. So, often we would head out straight from work to the boat – sometime just Stuart and us, or sometimes with other friends. The wonderful thing is – it doesn't get dark till 11 or so, and then only semi-dark. So you had many hours of cruising time available, even during the working week.

At weekends we could go even further afield. Sometimes we would come across a suitable looking little island and moor up for an hour or two. We'd light a fire on a chilly evening and take a beer or two. Did we swim? I don't think we ever did – the water would still have been icy from the winter. Then we would turn back west for home, into the setting sun. I can't remember it ever raining out on the water. But then the summers of one's youth are always warm and sunny.

7

Midsummer in Dalarna

After the excitement of Czechoslovakia and buying our boat, we then had Midsummer round the corner – yet more fun. Midsummer is a major event in the Swedish calendar. It's a tradition dating back to pagan times. It's celebrated on a weekend near to the summer solstice, towards the end of June. Friday and Saturday are 'red days' on the Swedish calendar – public holidays – and lots of places all over the country are closed the whole weekend.

It must be mentioned here that alcohol was a problem in Sweden. It was not uncommon to see a group of youths carrying plastic bags full of beer cans and rolling around the streets and T-bana platforms. Together with the noticeable lack of public toilets, this habit lead to a strong smell of stale urine in hidden corners around the city. Sweden was so liberal in many ways, yet there was (and still is) a strong

(back) Stevie, John, Stuart, Helena (front) Graham

temperance movement in the country. And it's well known that young people like to rebel against society's norms.

You could buy light and medium-strength beer (up to 3.5%) in supermarkets, but for stronger beer and wine and spirits, you had to go to one of the government-owned bottle shops which were managed by a national body known euphemistically as the *Systembolaget* (literally, the system company). At the time these shops were designed (you would think) to deter the buying of anything. There was no self-service, there were always queues and when you got to the counter, you were often faced with the grumpiest old crone you could imagine. There was a huge red light behind each crone with a notice telling you that if the red light came on, you had to show ID: you had to be over 21. You also had not to be on the 'black list' of barred customers – for misuse of alcohol. This light was supposedly random, but you knew that she pressed a button if you looked anything like under 25. And guess what? – the red light would often come on for us. But, who cared, it was all an experience. We didn't buy much alcohol anyway – just a few bottles of wine and maybe a bottle of aquavit now and again.

It wasn't only some young people who had a problem with alcohol. Pubs as we know them were not part of Swedish culture and most cafes in Sweden didn't sell alcohol. Of those that did, you had to buy some food, otherwise you couldn't buy a beer. Often you would see a solitary scruffy sad old bloke buying a beer and a sandwich. He would take the beer back to his table and leave the sandwich. This person might well be on the black list, so you might find him standing outside the *System*, offering you money as you went in and asking if you'd buy him a bottle of *brännvin* (spirit).

It's very different now. Although you can still only buy strong drink in the state-run monopoly shops, the shops are light and colourful and self-service and well-stocked and they have friendly, helpful staff.

Anyway back to Midsummer 1971. Then, as now, many people who lived in urban areas went back to their home town or village. They often had a *stuga* (summerhouse) there where all the family gathered.

A few of us decided to spend the long weekend in Dalarna, a region some 300km north-west of Stockholm, where Midsummer is celebrated even more traditionally than everywhere else. There were Helena, Stuart and his Swedish girlfriend Nicky, Peter, and also two university friends of ours, John and Stevie. We found a large house to rent for the weekend in a village called Röjeråsen, just north of the town of Rättvik.

So come Thursday afternoon, we set off in partial convoy heading north on the E18. It was exciting to be driving to and through somewhere we'd never been before. The Mini was still going strong, and we were together with John and Stevie in their Mini – it would have been unusual to see one Mini over there, never mind two in convoy.

After an enjoyable three hours or so we were getting near to Dalarna. We went through the industrial town of Falun. Falun gives its name to the ubiquitous dark red colour that so many Swedish houses are painted in – and particularly in Dalarna – because of its excellent preservative qualities. It's called Falu-red because the colour comes from a by-product of the copper mines in the area, mixed with rye flour and linseed oil.

Just down the road from where we were staying was the large lake Siljan, and the village of Vikarbyn. That was the site of many Midsummer activities, including maypole decoration and the raising of the pole from the horizontal to the vertical. Stalls and tombolas. Blonde women with flowers in their hair. The arrival of the 'priest boats'

Nyckelharpa

from outlying villages (look it up if you're interested). And music. Yes, the music which is so distinctive – performed by local people, all dressed in folk costume, playing fiddles and accordions and – a strange (to us) instrument called a *nyckelharpa* ('key harp'). It's a bowed string instrument with frets and piano-like keys, and you will see and hear them all over Sweden at Midsummer. (Some years later Helena actually made one of her own.) And the food – sill (pickled herring) (always the sill), boiled potatoes, sour cream, chives. Very tasty. Oh, and the ever-present *korv* (sausage) for those who couldn't go without it. But officially no alcohol – only what was optimistically called light beer (0.5%).

Two events stand out from that holiday – the first was the mozzies. We'd heard about them in rural Sweden, but in the autumn. Now, here we were in June, and there were plagues of them once the sun started to go down – even in the house. Maybe there were no mozzie screens on the windows and doors. They were always looking for a feed off human blood. They seemed to be attracted to certain types of skin (or was it blood?). Some people they went for, others they left alone. We were forever swatting them with a rolled-up newspaper. But it was a losing battle – you could never get them all. Judging from the state of the newspaper, they had a good feed off some of us before they got zapped.

The other thing that stands out in the memory is one evening's events – I suppose we'd eaten well and drunk a few *nubbar* (shots of aquavit) with a few beer chasers, and we were singing some rowdy songs, rugby songs they were, as Stuart was a rugby player. I remember something about a Frenchman going to the lavatory. At one point Stuart gets up on a low table and waves his arms around as if to conduct the tuneless rabble. The only problem was that he hadn't realised it was a glass-topped table. The inevitable happened: the glass shatters and Stuart's standing on the floor with razor sharp glass shards inches from his hairy legs, lucky not to have cut himself deeply. We however were reduced to falling about helplessly. I hope he owned up and paid to replace the glass.

John and Stevie came back with us to Stockholm. They'd brought us some things from England that we couldn't get in Sweden. Stevie, who was heavily pregnant, was sitting on the sofa unpacking packets of Shreddies and other such treats. Stuart comes up behind her. Looking fixedly at her cleavage in its low-cut summer dress, he utters the immortal words, 'And what goodies have you brought for Graham?' Maybe that's why his Swedish girlfriend called him Booby.

8

The end of the summer

The long days of summer passed and we spent many happy evenings sailing Belle out to the islands of the archipelago.

At the end of the summer you need to take your boat out of the water and put it up on *böcker* (trestles) somewhere on dry land. It was September by now. Stuart and Peter had left Sweden to work on projects elsewhere in the world. (In those pre-email days, it was much harder to keep in touch with ex-colleagues. We lost touch with Peter, although we did see Stuart in London a year or two later.)

So it was left to Wendy and me to arrange a winter resting place for Belle. I can't remember now, but I must have found this place somehow, maybe an ad in the paper. It was in a field in Åkersberga, a small town 30km north of Stockholm. I remember the rental on the patch of land was cheap, but maybe that was because it was several kilometres from the sea. So I needed to sail Belle from her mooring in Djurgården to a temporary mooring near Åkersberga, then get hold of a trailer to tow her by road to said field. It sounds quite a major project looking back all these years, but I didn't think twice about it then. Ah, the optimism of youth.

So, on the chosen day, I pick up Belle from her mooring and in a carefree fashion head off northwards, past Lidingö in the direction of Vaxholm – the trip should take about two hours. We'd hardly ever sailed to Vaxholm, a busy port both for local commercial ferries and for leisure craft. I was chugging along happily and I found myself in a large expanse of water east of Lidingö, with land a kilometre or two away, when the engine made some coughing noises and then stopped altogether. I remember thinking, oh dear, the engine's broken down. Looking back, a more likely explanation was that it had run out of fuel. I can't remember ever checking the fuel level – and I mean ever. Did I know *how* to check the fuel level? That was something 'the others' had done. I do remember stopping at a waterside filling station now and again to fill up with petrol, but I'd never thought to ask about checking the fuel level – either *fotogen* or petrol. Hmm, perhaps I should have done.

So there I was, bobbing gently up and down, the water slip-slapping on the hull in the silence, miles from land, with no other boat in sight. Was I worried? No, strangely. I was sure a small boat would pass by eventually. And, after a few minutes, one did. I waved my arms at it – the international distress signal – and it drew closer. It had a crew of one. When he got close enough, I shouted in my best Swedish, *'Bogsera?'* I knew that meant a tow. He nodded and said 'Vaxholm'. Well that was lucky. We soon got a line across and off we motored – well, he did.

Not long after, we were in Vaxholm. I thanked my rescuer. Did I buy him a beer? I hope so. So now the boat and I were in Vaxholm, and Wendy was waiting for me with the car in Åkersberga, some 25km away by road (less by water). A mobile phone would have been useful but they wouldn't be invented for another twenty-five years. I moored Belle in a temporary mooring and got a taxi to Åkersberga and the lay-up field. I asked the driver to take me to the address I'd been given – which for some reason I still remember – Malvavägen 44. When we got to said street, it turned out to be a long semi-rural street with hardly any houses and even fewer house numbers. We drove up and down a few times with no sign of number 44 – or of Wendy. Finally I spotted her walking up the street. Happily she wasn't cross, although by now it must have been much later than my ETA. Maybe she was pleased to see me. I was certainly pleased to see her.

Looking back, there's something wrong with this story, which the alert reader may have spotted. Why did we agree to meet at the lay-up field when I had no means of getting the boat there from the water which was several kilometres distant? I'm afraid I can offer no help on that question. But that is what happened.

Anyway we eventually found a field with a few boats on it, so that was clearly where we needed to get Belle to – but that was a job for another day. Again looking back, it was strange that the field was fenceless and gateless – it was an invitation for any budding villain to come and drive away with any or all of the boats on tow. Maybe even the unknown person to whom I'd posted a cheque for the space rental. But it turned out that that never happened – such was Sweden (and still is).

A few days later, I, with the help of friend George (of whom more later), borrowed a boat trailer and we went and picked up Belle in Vaxholm and took her to her winter resting place. The two of us somehow got her up on trestles, and covered her up with tarps and secured them with ropes. There to see out the freezing Swedish winter. Did I drain the engine of water, as I no doubt should have done? No I did not. Didn't even think about it.

Afterword: the following spring we went with two other friends to see if Belle was still there, and in what state she was. She was indeed still there and, apart from some flapping tarps, was as we had left her in the autumn. Our circumstances had changed and we knew that we wouldn't have use of Belle any more. Peter and Stuart had long since departed Swedish shores, and they had told us that they looked on what they had paid for Belle as a fair price for a wonderful summer of sailing in the archipelago, and they didn't expect anything back from an eventual sale. We thought the same, and who knew if the engine still ran?

So we told these two friends they could have her for nothing, and she was theirs if they wanted her. They did. 'Have you got the papers?' they asked, meaning registration documents. 'Papers? What papers?' I said. I'd never seen any papers. I expect Peter had them, and he'd gone off without even thinking about them. No doubt there should have been registration papers with the boat – Swedish officialdom ran on forms and paperwork. But hey – you don't knock back a free boat just because she doesn't have papers? That was the last time we saw Belle – hopefully she sailed for many more years.

As the nights drew in, we needed a winter sport to keep active. We both joined a squash club – the one at St. Eriksplan. Squash was hugely popular in Britain at this time – everybody played. It was popular in Sweden too, but easier to get a court. You just rocked up when you wanted a game, and put your name on the board. You didn't have to wait long. They had leagues and also knock-out tournaments. They were just starting up with women's tournaments. Wendy entered and won the first one! She won a squash racquet. The next time they had a tournament, they said she couldn't enter. How does that work? We never found out. Wendy did find out that the prize the next time was a generous IKEA voucher. She wasn't happy about that.

I was full of the spirit of 'give it a go' at that time – even for things that didn't come naturally to me – as may be apparent by now. One activity that our colleagues Vic and Malcolm were engaged in was amateur dramatics. There was a group called the Stockholm Players, which consisted mainly of transient Brits like us. Vic and Malcolm encouraged me to go along and see some rehearsals. So it was that one Sunday afternoon I rocked up at the small theatre in an alley called Yxsmedsgränd on Gamla Stan.

The play they were putting on was Tennessee Williams's *A Streetcar Named Desire*. After sitting through several rehearsals, I got to know a lot of the lines off by heart. I still remember some of them fifty years later – and hear them in my head:

'Stanley Kowalski – the lone survivor of the stone age'

'I have always relied on the kindness of strangers'

'Nothing belongs on a poker table but cards, chips and whiskey'.

Then came the day when they wanted somebody to play a bit part – at the start of the play there's a street vendor, who actually has lines. Two memorable lines in fact. I got the part. Me, who'd break out into a cold sweat at the thought of standing up in front of a group of people. But no, I wanted to try *everything*. And there was nobody else available. Could this be my big break?

Neither of my lines was hard to remember: the first was 'Red hot! Red hots!' I must have been selling something hot – chillis I supposed. In case the audience hadn't grasped the significance of the line, I got to say it again a few lines later, this time louder still: 'Re-e-ed h-o-o-t!' I soon got the hang of it in rehearsal – not that we rehearsed those early scenes much.

But that wasn't the end of it. There was also a part for a drunken sailor; he had no lines, but what he did have was a tottering stumble all the way from stage left to stage right, draped round the shoulders of a prostitute. I got that part too (the sailor, not the prostitute). This was clearly a more demanding role than the red-hot vendor, in that I only had actions to work with, no lines. I had no experience either of my profession or of my activity – I had to use my imagination (not one of my strong points). I wondered what the audience made of it.

The other players, it must be said, were brilliant – the parts of Stanley, Blanche, Stella and all the others. One of our cast members was Dennis Gotobed (yes really). About that time he had a part in the film *The Touch* starring Bibi Andersson, Max von Sydow and Elliott Gould. So now I could say I'd appeared with one of Ingmar Bergman's actors.

We played four nights to packed houses: it was a small theatre. The audience applauded fiercely at the end. We all took a bow. But I wasn't unhappy when our run ended. For some reason I wasn't invited back for any more productions. That was the end of my acting career.

One day in October 1971 we were having a quiet drink in the Tudor Arms when we met an Englishman called George. He was a much older man; we later found out that he was thirty-eight. In time we got to know George well and he was to play a part in our future. In fact we were to end up living in a room of his house. But for now we were chatting away and we said we worked with a few other English people in the IT business. George said he was in a similar line and that he worked for a large computer multinational.

After a couple of beers he said that he always had a Guy Fawkes Party out at his place in the country, and we and our colleagues were all invited. Guy Fawkes was unknown in Sweden, but we heard on the grapevine that there was a shop in Stockholm where you could buy fireworks, if you knew where to go. It turned out to be a small shop in a back street that sold various bits and pieces. They had a locked metal cabinet upstairs round the back. Within was a small selection of the usual fireworks, even rockets, and we invested in a few to take to the party. And so it happened that on November 5th, a few of us drove out to George's house for a Guy Fawkes party, just as we used to do back home. George's house was indeed deep in the country – some 50km north of Stockholm, over halfway to Uppsala.

His house was well away from the nearest town, surrounded by green fields and trees, an ideal place to let off a few fireworks and rockets without scaring people to death. We met George's Swedish wife Britta. There were a lively group there, both Swedes and English. The fireworks were let off and nobody got hurt. We had a few beers and then there was music and the dancing got quite energetic. Even our project leader, who was quite a placid fellow in the office, got in the party mood and was jumping around in a manic kind of way. And no, in case you're wondering, there were no drugs. This wasn't the sixties, was it? Smiley.

I'm pretty sure we didn't even have spirits, only beer and wine. Somebody must have had a camera as there are photos as evidence, one of which appears here, probably for the first (and last) time in a published form.

A good time was had by all. We must have slept in sleeping bags around the house. In the morning Britta cooked us all breakfast, English style. I do hope we paid something towards all George and Britta's hospitality – it must have cost them a fortune. We were to get to know George and Britta much better over the following months – more of that later.

Somebody mentioned that Duke Ellington and his world-renowned band were coming to play a concert in Uppsala in a few days' time. We didn't know anything about jazz but everyone had heard of the Duke, so we didn't want to miss the opportunity to see and hear them perform. We really enjoyed the concert and it was well received by the sell-out crowd. We learned later that a live LP had been recorded of the concert – which is still available today online. It's titled simply Uppsala 1971.

We both had been to Swedish lessons at LM's language lab earlier in the year – at no cost to us and during work time. We had a book called *Learn Swedish* and we listened to ourselves on headphones. I can still remember chapter 1 was all about pronunciation, and chapter 2 was about a chap called Herr Lundberg. He lived in a bedsit, he was poor and just had an old bike; he had an aunt who was very old and rich; he was always very friendly towards her. Two things of note here: the power of repetition –

after fifty years we can still remember these fifteen or so lines almost word for word; and secondly, the humour of these lines was never apparent at the time.

The LM lessons lapsed, or maybe we reached the end of the book. Now, at the start of autumn, I found another Swedish language course in the city. It was run by the Adult Education School (*Folkhögskola*), a national organisation which provides courses in many subjects for all, including immigrants. And, in our case, at no cost to the students. There were only five of us on the course, the teacher was really good, and we only spoke Swedish – not just because the students had different first languages. I so enjoyed those few months on that course, and I became a lot more confident in saying a few things in Swedish. One early evening I was driving to the course and it started to snow. It was the first snow of the year, and what was so striking for me was how huge the snow flakes were, and how quickly the snow settled. I'd never seen anything like it. Within a few minutes the road was covered in a thick layer of snow – in England the first snow turns to slush in no time at all.

Another memory from the course: one time we heard some angelic singing outside the door, as if in a dream. Then the door opens. An ethereal procession of whiteness enters the room; a dozen or so archetypally Swedish young women, wearing long white robes. The first girl was wearing a crown of lighted candles, and the girls following each held a lighted candle. And to complete

Neat row of bikes in Stockholm

the picture, they are singing a lilting song in Swedish, of which I catch the word *Lucia* ('Lu-chia'). This, we were told, was part of the annual Lucia day, celebrated each year on December 13th. The song was *Sankta Lucia*, a traditional song much heard at that time of year.

When the snow came in November, it stayed until the spring. It was a welcome sight too, as it helped to relieve the gloom of limited daylight. On a sunny day at the weekend we would sometimes drive out into the country, and the glistening snow on the fields and on the pine forests was spectacular. On smaller tracks in the country there were poles on the edges of the track every twenty metres or so to mark the way. Without them you would have no idea where the road was and you could easily find yourself stuck in a field. In the summer we had wondered what the poles were for; now we knew.

Clearing snow off the roads was clearly a routine job for the local authority: the snow ploughs were out on the highways within minutes. It might have taken a few hours to get to the less busy roads. Many drivers changed to studded tyres during the winter months. (It's now a legal requirement.)

It's especially icy on country roads first thing in the morning. Twice we skidded off the road on bends. Luckily no other vehicle was involved on either occasion, and there were no injuries. Once Wendy was driving, once me. Strangely enough we both said the same thing – the driver said it happened in a split second, the passenger said it happened as if in slow motion. The first time we were on a windy forest track, probably going too fast for the conditions and I lost it and we ended up half in the trees. We were able to extricate the car ourselves – just as well as we were miles from anywhere. The second time Wendy was on sheet ice near our house and we ended up in a deeper ditch. We had to ask our friendly landlord/farmer to tow us out with his tractor.

The snow turned our thoughts to skiing – another activity that was totally alien to us: only rich people went skiing in our experience. In Sweden everyone went skiing. But here's the thing – there are no mountains in southern Sweden, so it's not flash, look-at-me downhill skiing, it's cross-country skiing, or Nordic skiing – a totally different activity. You use your own energy to travel across mostly flat country, with the occasional small slope up or down. It's a lot quicker than walking, and requires less energy. The skis and boots are very different – for downhill skiing the boots are fixed rigidly to the skis, with one essential property: in the event of a crash, the boots (should) detach from the skis, with the result that you don't (shouldn't) break your leg or severely injure your knees. Cross-country skis on the other hand have most of the boot securely fixed to the ski, with only the heel free to move up and down. Using cross-country skis to go fast downhill is a sure recipe for major injury.

Unfortunately no one had told us that, before one Saturday we went to one of the big stores in Stockholm, with Helena in tow as the expert, to buy our ski gear. We came out the proud owners of skis, boots and no doubt a woolly bobble hat. The cross-country version that is, as they don't sell the downhill sort here. However, that didn't stop me looking for some steep hills in the countryside beyond Stockholm. Luckily (as it turned out) all I found were grassy mounds a few metres high, and we didn't get much above walking pace skiing down them.

One snowy day we had the benefits of Helena's local knowledge when we were out on the skis in the grounds of Drottningholm Castle, one of the royal palaces. It was freezing cold and we three had been out for a while. We'd covered a fair distance, but we'd never been told how to stop if you're going too fast downhill – which we were at one point. I soon found that the easiest way to stop is to bend your knees, keep your feet together and sit down. Wendy however decided to throw herself sideways onto the snow. But she got stuck. 'Help me!' she cried. 'Get the camera!' I called (so I'm told). But in due course I rushed to Wendy's rescue.

Helena knew of somewhere where she said we were sure of a warm welcome. Not far away, there was a wooden

Helena

cabin, with many pairs of skis leaning up outside. We left our skis with the others, and the ancient door creaked as we entered and our ski boots clopped on the old brick floor. We were met by the warmth of a blazing log fire and a room full of tables and chairs and rosy-faced skiers. That was when we discovered another Swedish delicacy – cloudberry jam (*hjortronsylt*) on a waffle freshly cooked over a wood stove. It really tastes fantastic – especially when you've got a cold face and a runny nose. It goes well with a mug of hot chocolate.

9

Helsinki weekend

Towards the end of 1971, it became clear that the SPL contract at LM Ericsson was coming to a close, and there was no talk in the corridors of another contract in Stockholm. What there was talk of, unofficially among the SPL people, was a possible contract coming up in Helsinki. The potential client was none other than Nokia – nothing to do with mobile phones of course, as they wouldn't be in common use for another twenty years.

Nokia had interests in many technological fields, and this project concerned software development in their banking business. This wasn't a contract SPL were pitching for; maybe too small for them. Our friends Tony and Pat (remember *My Sweet Lord*?) had a contract of their own at Nokia. There was work for more contractors, so they asked us if we were interested, and of course we said yes; if SPL didn't have work for us in Sweden at the end of the LM contract, we would be sent back to Nottingham, and we weren't ready for that just yet. So we were happy to talk to Nokia.

Nokia knew we were working full-time in Stockholm and that we couldn't come over during the week. No problem, they said, come over one weekend. And so it happened that one Friday evening in November, we boarded a Silja Line ferry in Stockholm bound for Helsinki. Another exciting adventure lay ahead. Eighteen hours on the water on a luxury boat, all expenses paid. What's not to like?

We got to Helsinki on Saturday morning, and as we disembarked, we suddenly thought, hey I wonder if we need passports? You don't normally need a passport to travel within the Nordic countries – you were never asked for a passport when travelling between Sweden and Denmark. But you did have to carry ID in case you were asked for it. All the foot passengers shuffled through Immigration with no-one even being asked to show ID. Then one of the immigration officers spots me, on the far side of the queue from him. He signals me over. Me? Why me? Maybe it was my jet black hair (yes really) and non-Nordic look. (Aside: it was not unknown if Wendy and I were together in a restaurant for the waiter to quickly realise I was not a native, and start speaking to Wendy – my assumed Swedish friend – in Swedish.) 'Where are you going?', he asks me in English. I tell him I live in Sweden and I'm going to Helsinki for the weekend. He relaxes when I tell him I live in Sweden. All sorts of weird people over there, he's thinking. 'ID please.' I didn't even have a driving licence with a photo on it – UK licences didn't have a photo then, strange as that was. But what I did have, luckily, was my Stockholm public transport pass, which had a photo together with my name and address. He was happy with that and waved me through.

Tony and Pat met us at the ferry terminal and drove us to their friends' house, where we would be staying on Saturday night. As we drove through Helsinki, we were struck by how different it was from a Swedish city. Different architecture and a clear Russian influence on the buildings; even churches with Russian-looking spires. Signposts with incomprehensible words on them; Finnish belongs to a different language group from the other Nordic languages. I learned later that it's one of the Uralic languages which include Hungarian and Estonian. The weather was dry and cold – about 0C.

Our house was modern and spacious and beautiful. There was a huge pine forest at the back of the house. In the afternoon we went to a trotting race, one of the national sports. Here the Russian influence was even more noticeable with gaunt, hard features on some of the faces, with the Russian-style fur hat much in evidence. We bet a few Finnish *markka* on some of the races, but we didn't win anything.

On Sunday morning we had our interviews with the Nokia people. They wanted to see us both together. There were two of them, male, not much older than us – friendly, good English. One of them wore a huge white polo-neck sweater which reminded me of Robert Shaw in *Battle of Britain*. Tony and Pat were there too. It was more like a discussion than an interview. We told them about what we were doing at LM, and they told us about their project. It all seemed to go well. 'We'll let you know.'

Afterwards, Tony and Pat took us back to the ferry terminal. We thanked them for looking after us so well. We said we hoped the meeting would have a positive outcome, as we both liked what we had seen of Helsinki and Nokia. There was that old allure of the unknown. But – it was not to be. Several weeks later we had a call from Pat – we didn't get the contract after all. She didn't say why – I suspect we may have been pitched too expensive, or maybe there were political problems. But we weren't too disappointed – by then we were happily installed in a different home and different jobs, which you will find out about if you read on.

10

Christmas in London

We were told by SPL that the contract at LM was finishing for all of us at the end of 1971. We would all be returning to our home SPL branches around the UK. A few days before Christmas, we cleared our desks, said our goodbyes to our Swedish colleagues and walked out of the door. We were to report to the SPL office in Nottingham when we got back.

We decided to take a few days leave and go back for Christmas. We packed all our meagre worldly possessions into the Mini – the kitchen table upside down on the roof rack – and all our other bits and pieces on the back seat and stuffed into dark corners that we never knew existed. This was a real test for the poor car's suspension, and the body looked a lot nearer the ground than was healthy for it. But we did get back to Gothenburg, and Tilbury, and finally to our flat in Nottingham. It was still there, just as we had left it twelve months previously. A lot of junk mail on the doormat. But otherwise cold and quiet inside. It felt very strange and foreign to be back. We caught up with some good friends. I did enjoy English pubs again – the beer and the atmosphere. That's one thing you don't get anywhere else in the world.

On the next working day we went into the SPL office in Nottingham. Wendy had worked there for several months before we left and knew most of the people. I had never worked there. Pretty soon we were both called into the manager's office. We had a feeling that all was not well. And so it turned out: there was no work coming up, either in the UK or abroad.

Thank you and goodbye. The boss had the grace to be apologetic about it, but he was no doubt under orders from above. We weren't too bothered, there would be other work to be found and we didn't have a mortgage to pay. In fact, we were free again – free to do whatever we wanted, to go wherever we wanted – a situation that life rarely affords you. We walked out the door and didn't look back.

I have to admit we hadn't lived frugally during most of our first year in Sweden – quite the reverse. Looking back, we could have saved a tidy sum to put towards a house deposit somewhere in the world. But no, life was to be lived and we made sure we did that. But we didn't buy a new car, we didn't go on fancy holidays (you couldn't call Czechoslovakia fancy), we didn't buy a new TV or record player or even records. But we had managed to spend a bit less than we earned towards the end of 1971. When we left Sweden at the end of the year, we closed our Swedish bank accounts. I walked out of the bank clutching a few crisp new 1000 kronor notes – worth £80 each. The largest denomination note in Britain then was £20. £80 was a fortune – it was my entire monthly salary the year before. In all it was enough to clear my student overdraft and still have enough to live on for the next few months.

We kept the Nottingham flat on as we didn't know where we would be living during 1972. It was like gold dust having a rented flat, and we didn't want to give it away unless we were sure. A few days before Christmas we motored south down the M1 to London to spend the holiday with Wendy's parents. It was good to see them again. And it was good to be young and free.

Part 2

1972 – 73 Droppsta

11

Down and out in Paris

As 1972 dawned we were thinking about what to do next. There we were in London staying with Wendy's Mum and Dad (Mick and Jack). We didn't want to be in the UK for more than a few days before April as we would then have been liable for UK income tax for the whole year. A lot of people in that situation wouldn't have worried about getting caught – and probably wouldn't have been – but we were too honest. It was winter and cold in Northern Europe, so we thought it would be a good idea to head south to Spain and some winter sunshine. There we could live cheaply for a few months and then think again about getting jobs – somewhere.

We packed a suitcase each and one morning in January, we headed for Dover and the Channel ferry. We planned to stay a few days with our friend Josiane in the Paris suburbs.

Josiane was my sister Jane's penfriend, and Jane and I had stayed a couple of times with her before.

We must have written to Josiane by letter to arrange our stay – even phoning abroad was almost unheard of then, not to mention hugely expensive. We duly arrived at her door. We only intended to stay with Josiane for a few nights so in our innocence we left our suitcases on the back seat of the car on the road outside. We made sure the doors were locked, so we were quite sure they would be safe. Then, as could have been foretold, disaster struck.

On our first morning there, I went out to the car and where there had once been two suitcases, now there was only emptiness. Oh what a blow. Car locks were notoriously insecure in those days – it would have taken a few seconds to force a Mini door handle open. So – everything was gone – we only had what we stood up in. A salutary lesson was learnt.

Josiane took us to the local police station to report the incident. We didn't really expect to get any of our stuff back but we wanted to tell somebody officially. The police station was straight out of Maigret, with shifty characters hanging around, world-weary gendarmes and the air thick with Gauloises. We eventually saw someone, and he gave us some *papiers*, signed and stamped.

Now it seemed just too hard to follow our original plan and head down to Spain. It would be a new, foreign country for us and we felt ill-equipped to deal with that. As it was, the best thing to do was to go back to our recent home Stockholm. Josiane said it was a very exciting idea to drive to Sweden, and I agreed. I think she would have liked to come too.

And so it was that one morning towards the end of January 1972, we packed up all our worldly possessions – down to a packet of Prince cigarettes and a toothbrush by now. We headed north from Paris, not south as we had originally intended. It was a sunny morning, and I was happy to be going back to familiar territory, and I think Wendy was too. It was as if the break-in had soured the whole Spain adventure. Maybe we weren't meant to go to those unfamiliar Mediterranean places.

It's almost 2000km from Paris to Stockholm with at least one ferry on the way. Our navigation aids consisted of a road atlas. We knew there was a ferry from Amsterdam to Gothenburg – but we didn't know when it sailed – hopefully every day. So we headed to Amsterdam – a 500km trip from Paris. Through northern France, a bit of breakfast on the autoroute, through Belgium. If it's Tuesday this must be Belgium, I thought to myself. Into Holland, stopping at each border in those days, getting another stamp in the passport.

We eventually got to Amsterdam docks, only to find that there wasn't a ferry to Gothenburg for two days. Why didn't we go to a travel agent in France to find out the ferry times? That would have been too sensible I suppose – more fun to find out when we got there? Possibly, I'm not sure after all this time.

We had been on the road for at least eight hours, but we definitely didn't spend a night in a hotel, or anywhere else. We just kept driving, one sleeping or dozing while the other one drove. Our next target was Travemünde on the north German coast – we knew there was a ferry from there to Trelleborg in Sweden. Another 550km from Amsterdam to Trelleborg, heading east to the German border, then on the autobahns of northern Germany.

After many hours, we arrived at Travemünde docks, tired but still high on adrenalin. It was early evening, and dark already in January. As luck would have it, they were just loading the last few cars on to the ferry. What a bit of good fortune. We didn't have a ticket of course, and we couldn't see a ticket office anywhere. So we joined the end of the line of cars being loaded and when we got to the chap collecting tickets, he looked to check ours. *'Wieviel?'*, I ask him in my best school German. How much? He looks surprised, thinks for a moment, then *'Zwanzig Mark'*. Twenty Marks. Wow, a winner! It should have cost much more than that. So I hand over a twenty Deutschmark note and he pockets it, looking happy. We drive up the ramp, and there's just enough space for a small car. How lucky was that – again.

We find our way up to the bar/restaurant. The boat is half-empty and there are lots of spare seats. We eat and drink hungrily. There are a few other folk around, and before long the beers are flowing and there's music playing and everyone's up on the dance floor jumping around.

These Swedes are very lively. Maybe they're German – but unusual for Germans to be travelling to Sweden in January. Another thing strikes me – all the signs around the walls are in Danish and German. Then it dawned on me – this boat's not going to Sweden, it's going to Denmark.

Well never mind, Denmark's sort of in the right direction, but it just means we've got an extra few hundred kilometres to drive, and another ferry from Copenhagen to Malmö. It's also a much shorter crossing – four hours – not the eight hours to Trelleborg, so less sleep time. We stretched out on some padded bench seats and got a bit of sleep. It must have been about midnight when we docked in Denmark – this must be Gedser, I reckoned. It was. The night air was cold: we were travelling further north all the time.

The Mini was still not missing a beat, remarkable really, it wasn't built for epic journeys like this. Thank goodness for that too – it wouldn't have been much fun in the middle of nowhere in the middle of the night with a defunct motor.

So, more hours through the sleeping Danish countryside, to Helsingør and the short ferry ride across to Helsingborg in Sweden. Ah, this looks familiar, even though we'd never been there before: a Swedish building is unmistakably a Swedish building. Strange how a country has a distinctive look, even a city you've never been to before. Now only 560km left to go to Stockholm.

It was the middle of the night and it was freezing cold. There wasn't so much motorway in those days, and it was a lonely long journey as the kilometres ticked down ever so slowly. We were still taking turns behind the wheel or alternatively having a doze. No cruise control then, and I'd give my right leg a rest by using my left foot on the throttle for long stretches. There was thick snow all around but, being a main route, the road was clear of snow. We stopped at one of those sparklingly modern roadside cafes they have in Sweden, for coffee and food and warmth. It was beside Lake Vättern, one of the two huge lakes in the middle of Sweden. As we got out of the car and the cold air hit our lungs, I saw that there was thick ice on the front of the wing mirrors and the bonnet. The car too was more black than blue, covered in the salty road spray that you get driving over there in winter. But it was good to be back in Sweden: it felt like home. Perhaps the break-in in Paris was meant to be.

Finally there was light in the eastern sky and we found ourselves in the outskirts of Stockholm. Here was the whole city spread out before us. Where shall we go? We didn't have a home there any more. There was no choice really: it had to be to Helena. Did we phone her to tell her we were on our way? Probably not. Helena had an apartment on Värtavägen in Gärdet overlooking a large park.

Helena was surprised to see us again, but then again probably not that surprised. She had a cool one-bedroom apartment and she let us stay in her living room and we slept on the sofa. We had no home and no jobs. No clothes either, come to that. Were we downhearted? No we were not.

We had endless possibilities. We had a few crowns in our pocket. And we were in a beautiful city, with spring around the corner.

We were sure of one thing. We were meant to be in Sweden, not Spain.

We went to the Tudor Arms one day and we bumped into George. Fireworks George that is, George from Droppsta. We were recounting our recent adventures and how we were staying temporarily with Helena. George says, 'Hey why don't you come and stay with us, we've got a spare room upstairs.' Sounds good, why not? And so began a new chapter in our young lives.

12

Not so Dynamic Data

If you remember, George worked as a technical writer. He had a round face and a ready smile. He had a hint of a West Country accent. He lived with his Swedish wife Britta in the old schoolhouse near a farm, deep in the countryside not far from historic Sigtuna, between Stockholm and Uppsala. Britta's family owned and ran the farm, which was called Droppsta Gård ('Gord'). George and Britta had modernised the old schoolhouse into a comfortable home. There was a spare room upstairs which they generously said we could use for the time being. We thought we would take up the offer for a week or two, find a job for at least one of us, then move out into our own place.

George was a bit of a dreamer, not really happy I think with working in an office, and always on the lookout for an entrepreneurial scheme. One day George came up with

George

an idea: why don't we set up a computer software business? His thinking would have been: these two young folk are working in IT – therefore they must be able to do any type of computing assignment that comes along.

The (unwritten) deal was that we got board and lodging with George and Britta, and we would look round for some data processing work. Britta worked at a small business nearby where they had a basic Honeywell card-processing computer – tiny in terms of today's processing power, but this was 1972. The manager there was amenable to us using his computer in the evenings and at weekends. Presumably he got something out of the deal – maybe he thought we would be on-the-spot trouble-shooters should anything go wrong with his set-up? (Luckily it didn't.)

Full of the optimism of youth, this sounded like an excellent plan to us, so one day in January we moved all our stuff – very little after our two suitcases had disappeared in Paris – from Helena's flat in Stockholm to the old schoolhouse. We were soon installed and it was good to be in a warm and well-insulated house. We had the cosy room upstairs where we installed a large tabletop as an office desk, and tried to look the part. Our office equipment consisted of a pad of paper, sharpened pencils, coding sheets, a pad of print layout sheets and a stapler. We must have had a Honeywell programming manual as well, for our card-driven, no hard drive or mag tape, mickey mouse computer. There was even a phone downstairs that we could use. We were ready to conquer the world.

We thought we had better set up a company, just in case somebody paid us some money. But you needed at least one Swedish person as a director. Well, Britta's Swedish, she wouldn't mind, would she? I think she was used to George's mad schemes, and she agreed. Then we had to think of a name for our fledgling company. We eventually came up with – Dynamic Data. Britta filled in the forms, somebody wrote a cheque for a few hundred kronor, and soon after we got back in the mail a certificate stating that we were now Dynamic Data AB.

We got some business cards printed, nothing fancy, just the company name, address and phone number. When they came back we thought they were really flash; however somebody was later heard to say that it was the least dynamic business card he'd ever seen. He was right, of course.

All we needed now were some clients. George had an English friend John, who had lived in Sweden for a few years so his Swedish was pretty good. He was brought on to the sales team – in his spare time. No, he *was* the sales team. Together we nutted out a one page sales letter (in Swedish) – we offered programming and processing services. In those days it was the norm for businesses to buy tailor-made software – the time of packaged software was a long time off. From a market research firm, we bought the names and addresses of a few hundred possible customers, and posted them our sales blurb. Oh yes, we were professional, even if we didn't expect much response from our simple flyer, to be honest.

I'm finding it hard to write this, but I rang up some of these prospects on cold calls. Yes, in my best Swedish. Really. No one was rude to me or slammed the phone down, which says a lot for Swedish tolerance. I even understood what they said but I don't suppose I ever got past the receptionist. So I didn't get any business. I would have been stunned if anyone had seriously responded.

At other times we studied the Honeywell programming manuals – it would have been a very simple high-level language – remember there were no disc drives or mag tapes or other online storage. Just punched cards. What serious application could anyone develop on this simple machine? What *were* we thinking?

Imagine our surprise when one day we got a phone call from somebody who was interested in our services. He said his name was Benny and he ran a motorcycle dealership and he wanted a computer system to handle his spare-parts stock control. This was the break we'd been waiting for.

It was also the start of a long involved saga, which is too long (and depressing) to relate fully here. The executive summary: Wendy and John went to talk to Benny at his business. He seemed like a genuine bloke and his business looked busy. He was no doubt struck by this young Swedish-looking Englishwoman. Benny showed them his manual system for recording his spare-parts inventory – rows and rows of card indexes. There were thousands, probably tens of thousands of different spare parts. Alarm bells should have been ringing for us.

But no – *'Inget problem Benny. Det här klarar vi väl!'* (No problem Benny, we can sort this out.) We must have talked money, but I can't remember what we agreed. But we got the job! I'm sure we didn't even have a contract or a specification. I know Wendy and I spent many hours, days and weeks borrowing boxes of index cards, taking them back with us and transferring all the parts information onto punched cards. We will never forget the Swedish for nut (*mutter*) and bolt (*bult*).

We designed an order form on continuous stationery for Benny to order new stock from his supplier, which he got printed by the thousand. We wrote some code. After a month or so, we started to wonder, is this ever going to work? The answer was, of course – no it wasn't. Even if we'd got all the programs written, how was he ever going to provide us with the input on an ongoing basis? How were we ever going to process it on our toy computer? There was nothing for it – we had to tell Benny.

There was no way of breaking it gently. Well, he took it pretty well. He must have been having his doubts anyway. He didn't threaten to sue us. He'd only paid us a small interim payment, but he'd spent on the stationery (which he could still use with another system provider) and we'd wasted a lot of his time. But, on the plus side, he had a few thousand punched cards with his spare parts master file, which he may have been able to use in the future. He must have thought: well, I'm not making that mistake again – I'll do my due diligence next time. In that sense it was a lesson he learned quite cheaply, on the scale of IT disasters.

And a lesson for us too of course. But were we daunted? Did we learn a lesson? Would we do our due diligence next time? Oh no. Dynamic Data AB's next project was even more doomed to failure.

We were relieved to be shed of the Benny project that had been hanging over our heads for months. Before the next project reared its ugly head, I sort of fell into a job that I really enjoyed.

We'd both spent a lot of time at Britta's company using their computer, and we'd got to know some of their staff, including the manager. One day Britta said they needed somebody part-time to drive their van to and from Arlanda, Stockholm's main international airport, which was only 10km from Märsta. This sounded like a fun job, so I said I'd give it a go. It was only for a few hours a week and the pay would have been minimal. I only had a UK driving licence but nobody asked to look at it. I didn't even have an interview – somebody threw me the keys to the VW Transporter and said off you go.

Britta explained where exactly I had to go at the airport and what to do. I was to go into the internal offices, beyond the public area. Did I need security clearance to work at an airport? No I didn't, and I was never asked for ID. I didn't have a lanyard round my neck either. That's how it was in those days.

There were a few smallish parcels to deliver to the freight company. I really enjoy getting to know a new place, even if it's just a new building at an airport; especially at an airport. As I may have mentioned, I love how quickly the human brain gets to recognise a new place, so it instinctively registers if something's different from the last time, even something small like signage. It's those neurons and synapses again.

Often there would be packages to pick up and take back to our office. I really liked being out on the back roads and the feeling of doing something useful and not having a care in the world. Very soon you can drive the route without thinking about it, which makes it very relaxing and almost a kind of meditation.

Dynamic Data AB was still a legal entity, and both Wendy and I and George still had vague hopes that we could do something profitable with it. However our next wacky scheme would go the same way as the Benny motorbike project disaster.

One of the big trends of the early 1970s was computer dating – the Tinder of its day. There were three or four companies in the UK that were making big money from this new scientific way of meeting people. Each of these companies had a computer somewhere (supposedly) but the whole operation relied on the postal system. It seems so slow now. But things *were* a lot slower in those days. The way it worked was: you sent off for an enrolment form, you filled in some facts about you and your interests, and then there were questions about what type of person you were looking for. Then you posted it all back to the dating company. They would feed all that into their state-of-the-art computer, it would rumble away for a while, then it would print out the names of likely compatible partners – who didn't live at the other end of the country. So, a hugely complicated operation, open to all sorts of problems – there not being any other clients near you – let alone *suitable* clients, privacy issues, us getting sued by unhappy clients, to name a few.

And that was in Britain, a far more densely populated country than Sweden. Was it any surprise that computer dating hadn't hit Sweden? No it wasn't. Sweden, with its scattered population – people living in towns hundreds of kilometres from the next town, in some cases. We said to each other, well Sweden's a large and far-flung country – they'd *love* computer dating. It really is hard to believe now that we didn't realise that computer dating wouldn't make it any less large and far-flung. And it's hard to believe that we thought we could even scrape the surface of this probably non-existent market. But that's what we did think.

The first thing we needed was a form for the clients to fill in. Why not 'borrow' somebody else's? So we sent off for a form from one of the leading UK dating companies. It soon came back – so we could see exactly what information was requested, and how the form was laid out. All we had to do now was translate it into Swedish, and get it printed. The translation part wasn't hard – Britta looked after that. We thought we could fit all the information on a folded A4 sheet of paper – smaller than the English form we were cribbing from.

George said he could get it printed at the place he worked, where they had state of the art printing technology – some kind of Magic Typewriter. What this miracle machine did was typeset a document, with selectable fonts and justified text – features which today any word processing app can do at little or no cost. George used this machine in his daily work, but he thought it would be useful to have one of us with him. It would have been too obvious if we'd gone into his office on a weekday, so George says, no problem, we can go in at the weekend.

And so it was that one Sunday morning, George and I set off in the Spitfire to get to work on 'our' form design. I remember it clearly: it's strange how there are some seemingly unimportant scenes that stick in your head, even from fifty years ago. On the way there, we needed to refuel and we pull in to a petrol station on a back road into Stockholm. George liked back roads. It's an old-fashioned place where they pump the petrol for you. BBC World Service is on the car radio playing that bit of music they have before the news. Then into my head flashes a scene straight put of Bergman's *Smultronstället* (Wild Strawberries). The pump attendant, wearing overalls and a weathered face, comes out to fill up and has a few words with the driver. The pump attendant is surely Max von Sydow. (Herr Professor Borg wasn't driving a Spitfire however.) What's more, that film was about the character's memory of his early years and contained many flashbacks to his childhood.

Soon after, George and I are at his plush offices in the northern suburbs of Stockholm. George has a swipe card that opens the door – and it doesn't care how many people go in. The Magic Typewriter that cost a fortune and was way beyond the means of home users, was sitting there waiting for something to do. It did indeed look like a giant typewriter. In spite of its abilities it turned out to be an incredibly slow and fiddly process. You had to type a few words in, and then the machine would work out how many words it could get on the first line – then you had to adjust the spacing millimetre by millimetre to get it to justify the line. Each line took minutes. And then there were the boxes – where the client could put a tick or leave it blank – even fiddlier than the text.

One of George's colleagues stuck his head round the door, and looked surprised when he saw a stranger (me) not looking like a typical client. But he left without comment. After a few hours, the entire document was finished – one double-sided A4 sheet. It looked horrible – like a first term high-school project – 'amateur' did not do it justice. And in black and white (colour was out of the question). But you could still see its heritage: it bore some resemblance to its UK ancestor that we had borrowed it from. It was incredibly cramped – the font was too small and the spaces to fill in the answers were much too small. But it was the best we could do with our limited resources. We never considered getting it printed by a print bureau. We ran off a few hundred copies on the photocopier.

Meanwhile Wendy started on the massive task of writing the programs to process the hundreds (thousands?) of punters' forms we were expecting. All we needed now were the punters. We didn't want dissatisfied clients banging on our front door, and a personal address didn't look professional, so we got a PO box number from the post office.

What to call our revolutionary product? After an extensive focus group study (that is, the four of us having a quick chat) we decided on Data Date: English, with the allure of the foreign, but easily understandable by the target market.

Now for our advertising campaign. Before we went national we thought we should test the local market. One afternoon George and I drove up to Uppsala University, and wandered around the central buildings until we came across a building that looked like the Students Union. There we found some large notice boards with the usual Flat To Rent etc. ads flapping on scruffy bits of paper. We borrowed some drawing pins and stuck up a few of our modest Data Date application forms. I suppose we didn't look like students, but we escaped unchallenged. Nothing ever came of this marketing campaign, of course.

But now to hit the national market; there were two national tabloid newspapers with large circulations – *Expressen* and *Aftonbladet*. We plumped for one of them, and designed a large display ad. It would have cost a considerable amount from our non-existent budget to place it. It was lucky the paper didn't want a story out of it: we would have been exposed as the incompetent amateurs that we were before we'd got to first base.

The ad duly appeared one day – at the top of a right-hand page. We looked at it in amazement and wondered at our brazen enterprise. Surely there must be some response to our huge advert? A couple of days later I opened our post office box and – dozens of envelopes fell out – yes handfuls. I quickly gathered them up, and took them back to Data Date corporate HQ. George was beside himself with excitement – he could see a life of luxury ahead – fast cars and yachts on the Riviera. We counted how many there were – fifty or so that first day. But, as expected, day one was the biggest day for replies

– the following days the post tailed off miserably. It was immediately clear that we didn't have nearly enough responses to enable us to provide a meaningful matching service for our clients. We had about seventy people scattered over the vast area of Sweden – and guess what? – many more men than women. And no, it wasn't even a thought in those days to ask if you were looking for a same-sex partner.

We didn't ask for any money from the client until we'd made an 'introduction'. Even if we'd made introductions for half of our respondents, our income would have been like loose change – certainly less than our expenditure. My fears about the poor quality of our application form were confirmed when we read the completed forms – we hadn't left nearly enough space for people to write in, or tick boxes.

In short, it was another Dynamic Debacle.

We still felt a commitment to our expectant clients even though they hadn't paid us anything. With the number of people we had on our books, a computerised solution was unnecessary; no, worse than that, impossible. But it was clear from looking at the forms for a few minutes and putting them in county piles that our clients were incompatible, scattered as they were over this huge country. Let's quickly draw a veil over this fiasco – it all died a death.

At least it should have died a death; George found a way of prolonging the agony. He thought it would be interesting to meet the man behind the UK dating company whose form we'd plagiarised. Yes, really. So he wrote and invited him over to meet with us. What on earth did we have to offer him? I honestly can't remember. To our great surprise this highly successful UK businessman wrote back and said, 'Thank you, yes I'd love to come and meet you.' Maybe he thought, a) I can expand my empire by taking over these Swedish amateurs and b) I'll meet some charming Swedish women.

So, one day not long after, he arrives at Arlanda, and we pick him up. He's called James and he's a pleasant chap – no doubt totally bemused as to who he's going to meet. He's in his thirties, fair, not tall, intelligent, not brash. We show him 'our' form – the one we stole from him and put into Swedish. His expression doesn't change, to his credit and my relief. We had a chat about our common business, but it must have been clear to James within a few minutes that we were of no possible interest to him. He didn't appear put out, or in any way negative towards us, and his visit became social rather than business. George lent him his Spitfire for the day and off he went. Maybe to Stockholm and more rewarding, or pleasurable, activities. Who knows? The next day we took James back to Arlanda, and off he flew, no doubt to continue his successful business in the UK, shaking his head at the strange things people do.

After the Data Date debacle, all of us, even George, realised that Dynamic Data AB wasn't going to make us our fortune. It was time to put it out of its misery. We were wiser and not a lot poorer. I resolved to get on with the more practical business of earning a living as an employee and leading a more normal life.

13

Burroughs

Going back to January of this year, 1972, we moved into the upstairs room at Droppsta and one of us (at least) needed to find a job: we realised Dynamic Data AB wouldn't be generating any income in the near future. I'd put a short notice in the classified section of *Dagens Nyheter* (Daily News) Situations Wanted, but nothing came of that.

Every day I'd check the Jobs pages in DN as well. There were always several IT jobs advertised, but they were usually looking for specific experience – often on IBM 360 systems, and neither of us had that. When applying for a job in Sweden, it was the norm to include a *betyg* (reference) or two together with your covering letter and CV. And it was the norm for an employer to give you a *betyg* when you left a company, requested or not. So we had a reference each from SPL – and in Swedish. They were positive – that's all that mattered.

I had access to a typewriter, the technology of the day, so I was able to produce a professional-looking application. But it took quite some time to write a covering letter for each new application, and maybe tweak the CV.

One day in February I was at George's when I got a call from somebody at Burroughs in Stockholm. I had applied to their ad several weeks previously, and I didn't really expect to hear from them after that long. Burroughs Machines Ltd was a major computer manufacturer, one of a small number of companies that had a share of the market that was left after IBM, by far the major player, had taken their huge share.

Burroughs was a US company that had started in cash registers and other office equipment many decades earlier. Now they produced a range of small business computers, going up to the largest of mainframes.

I was invited for an interview. Their office was near Karlaplan in Stockholm, and was the Swedish head office for the company. The journey from Droppsta took about an hour – ten minutes drive to Märsta station, thirty minutes on the *pendeltåg* (suburban train) to T-centralen, four stops on the T-bana to Karlaplan. The office was on a wide pleasant street that ran from Karlaplan down to the water at Djurgården. I thought, this would be a good place to work.

The systems manager was called Ingmar. He was OK. I appeared to be the only candidate today. We had a bit of a chat – in English. The thing was, all the Burroughs documentation was in English, and you needed to be able to understand that. The role of the company was to sell hardware: mostly small office computers that sat on a desk, and the occasional mainframe once in a blue moon. But a computer was of no use without software. (In those days nobody outside the industry had ever heard of software. I had many discussions with people trying to explain what software was. 'Well it's like the music that a musical instrument – the hardware – plays' was one of my analogies. Seems strange now.)

There were some off-the-shelf software packages for standard accounting functions – invoicing, creditors, debtors, general ledger, payroll were the common ones – but by far the most usual practice was for the customer to buy tailor-made programs. This was the job that Burroughs were recruiting for; they had a team of six in this role.

After my chat with Ingmar, he says we'd like you to do a psychological test – what we would call an IQ test. Well I love all that sort of stuff. It was a multiple choice test, with shapes and patterns and odd men out etc. There were more questions than anyone could answer in the allowed time, but I didn't panic. I think that's the main thing, not to panic. Just do what you can. I thought I hadn't done too badly.

So the next thing they have lined up is an interview with two of the salesmen. This time it's in Swedish. This didn't bother me too much – I'd been there over a year, and although all the work at LM had been in English, I felt the evening classes had been a lot of help, and I'd read the local newspapers a lot (as I do).

They were business-like and not unfriendly, and all they really wanted to know was whether I could understand a program spec. This was what the salesperson wrote after finding out the customer's requirements. They had a sample invoicing spec to go through with me. A lot of it was in diagrammatic form, so that was no problem. I had a common sense idea of what an invoicing program does, even though I'd never written one. I asked a few questions, which they seemed to be reassured by.

Then one of them leans back and says, '*Vad har Ni för lönekrav?*'. Well, that wasn't an everyday expression, but luckily I picked it up. What are your wage requirements? Always a promising sign to be asked about money. I'd thought of a figure – way less than I had been getting as a contractor at LM, and based on what I'd seen offered in adverts. And now I'd be paying Swedish tax, known to be as high as anywhere in the world. I ventured 2400 (£200). A month. It's always monthly. He nodded. So that was OK.

A few days later I got a letter offering me the job. I was really happy about that, and Wendy was too of course – finally some money coming in. A real job in Stockholm, paying real Swedish taxes, going on a real Swedish train every day! What's not to like? And at the 2400 I'd asked for. The letter went on to say that I'd have to put in an invoice every month for that amount. Ingmar later explained that they were only allowed by the US head office to employ a certain number of programmers. So I was hidden as some other expense. It didn't matter to me as long as I got paid. Did I ask about hours of work, holiday pay, sick pay? Apparently not.

When I told George I'd got a job, he said, 'Hey that's great', but I did wonder if he meant it. And so began the Burroughs months. Wendy drove me to the station every morning through the ice and snow. The train started at Märsta, my station, so I always got a seat. I enjoyed getting the train in the mornings, and it wasn't that small a train that you were always sitting next to the same people: I couldn't have coped with that. Not that Swedes are in the habit of talking to strangers. I'd buy a *Dagens Nyheter* at the *Pressbyrån* (kiosk) and happily read that on the half-hour journey to T-centralen. Then a five-minute walk to the T-bana to catch a Ropsten-bound train. And the short walk from Karlaplan.

Wasn't this an expensive trip daily? Well, no. They'd just introduced the 50-card in Stockholm – a very Swedish concept which they should have everywhere. What is it? You get a card, on which you write your name and address and person number (a number every Swedish person has – you can't do anything without it), attach an ID photo to it, and then each month you buy a sticker for (only) 50 crowns. Then you can travel free on any public transport in greater Stockholm – even out as far as Märsta. 50 crowns a month is very little, so you get to think of public transport as being free. You don't have to use a 50-card, you could pay for a single journey, but that's expensive, so why would you do that?

I really enjoyed my job – although I dug a hole for myself at one stage. There were five other people in the programming group, and we all got on well. My Swedish came along in leaps and bounds – especially the everyday words. Every day about lunchtime, somebody would get up and say, '*Dags att käka!*' (time for some grub). At the end of the day, it would be, '*Dags att åka hem!*' (time to go home). We each worked on our own job, which usually took about a month or two. The L2000 series computers were nice machines to work on, and it wasn't a problem to find a spare machine to test on. The programs were either written in a medium-level assembler language, or in COBOL on the L7000 machines.

The usual storage was magnetic cards – a card about the size of an A4 sheet of paper, with a magnetic stripe running down the side from top to bottom. You could store 256 characters on a card. We punched the programs up ourselves on 80-column cards. The cards were then read in on a mainframe and compiled. The mainframe output the compiled program onto 5-hole paper tape. Sometimes the paper tape punch would throw a wobbly and omit to punch a hole. We got quite adept at reading the paper tape, finding the missing hole and hand-punching it, or covering up an extra hole with a patch.

The office computer, as well as having a magnetic card reader, had a keyboard, a golf ball printer, and a small amount of solid state memory. There was a special Swedish golf ball with the extra Swedish letters on it – Ä, Ö and Å, and their lowercase versions. It's surprising the range of applications that you can process with that modest configuration.

I started at Burroughs in February 1972. There continued a pattern that was to recur repeatedly in my IT career – I took on too much. And I should have asked for help. My first project involved a quite complex invoicing program – discounts for certain customers, products with a complicated pricing structure etc. But after six weeks or so, the program was ready and tested and it was punched onto paper tape and posted off to the customer, who was in a provincial city – Karlstad I remember. I had many calls from the office manager, Lena, with various queries (in Swedish) about why something worked the way it did, and we had a good understanding. She was happy with the program and spent a lot of time setting up all the product files and customer files etc.

Sometimes there was a small change needed, so I'd make the change, punch out a new program on paper tape and post it off to her. Then later I wouldn't hear from her for days at a time, and I got on with the next project. Then one day she rings up and says that it's made a mistake. I really wanted to find out what was going wrong – and so did she of course – so I started working late. It was easier to run and test the new program in the evenings when the office was empty. It was just me in the deserted office on many evenings. Often, if I felt like some fresh air, I'd walk down to Strandvägen to the Pressbyrån on the corner and ask for *Två små Lift*. (two small bottles of orange juice). An interesting cultural difference: you weren't expected to say please – but you *were* expected to say *varsågod* when you gave them the money – a silent transaction back home. In fact there is no Swedish word for *please*, as we use it. Similarly there's no English word for *varsågod* – it literally means 'be so good'.

Often Lena would need the new program the next day, so I arranged with our office staff that I could use the franking machine to print a postage label. Then, as long as I posted the package before 9pm at the post office up the road, it would get to Karlstad (300km away) the next day. I'd ring Wendy up and tell her what train I'd be catching. She'd be waiting for me at Märsta station. It was often late evening by the time I got home.

Some days there be no call from Lena for a few days, so I'd be thinking, I must have fixed it. Then she'd call and say that it had gone wrong again. Then she gave me a clue: 'It only happens when I start a new magnetic card.' Ah ha! Then I twigged finally what was going wrong. If only I'd asked for a second pair of eyes to look at the problem, it would have saved the customer a lot of trouble, and me a lot of hours, and a lot of packages to Karlstad. Lena for her part was remarkably patient.

A few weeks later Ingmar and I went on the train to Karlstad one day for a meeting with the customer, largely as a PR exercise. So I finally got to meet Lena, which was nice; we'd spoken so much on the phone. We had a good day there, and the customer was happy, which was the most important thing.

A few months later a customer in Malmö wanted some changes to his program (ie my program) and Ingmar decided that the best solution was for me to go down to Malmö for a few days to see for myself what was required. As it turned out, I went down several times. As you now know, we lived only ten minutes from Arlanda airport, so it was only a short trip for Wendy to drive me over in the cold dark morning to get the 7am SAS flight to Malmö. There was no such thing as a security check in those days, and no passport control on a domestic flight, not even an ID check. A paper ticket was all you needed. We boarded quickly and in no time at all we were airborne. The rain was streaming down the windows and the weak winter sun was coming up. Coffee came round very soon and it tasted good. It was only an hour's flight to the brand new Malmö airport at Skurup. It was well known as an example of modern Swedish architecture: it was painted in many bright colours, inside and out. Very Sweden in the seventies. For me it was another huge excitement.

I went to the Burroughs office in Malmö every day. It was staffed by salesmen and engineering staff – no programmers – or saleswomen come to that. Even in progressive Sweden, there were few women in sales generally. (Although it was noticeable that there was more gender equality here. Women even played football.)

One other thing stands out for me – every day at 5.30 precisely, not a minute earlier or later, all the salesmen would get up from their desks and go downstairs to the canteen. Strange! There, the fridge was opened, and an array of beers stood in serried ranks. The beers were handed round and popped and everyone heaved a sigh of relief as the cold beer hit their parched throats. The manager in particular looked old and tired and stressed all day long – I got the impression he was hanging out every day for 5.30 to come around – and maybe also retirement day.

After I'd been there a few days I'd got to know Kim, one of the salesmen, quite well. He was a friendly chap, and he said, 'Why don't you ask your wife down for the weekend, and you can stay with us?' So I rang Wendy and suggested it: hey yes, she liked that idea. Burroughs paid for her air fare – the same for them as paying for me to go home for the weekend. Kim and his wife made us very welcome. We hadn't been to Malmö before, so it was fun to have a look around. One day we went on the ferry across from Limhamn to Copenhagen; it took an hour and a half. It was coming up to Easter and the custom in Skåne (the south-western region where we were) was to eat goose at this time. So the four of us enjoyed a roast goose meal on the ferry. It was something we hadn't eaten before – very tasty it was with all the trimmings. I do hope we paid the bill for the four of us.

Wendy flew back home after the weekend. I was still needed for another week or so; one day they asked me to hop over to the Burroughs office in Copenhagen. So it was back on the ferry, and a change of scenery for a few hours. It was interesting to see a little bit of Denmark, and another Burroughs office. I had no Danish, so we must have used English. It wasn't long after that I was back on the ferry to Malmö. I remember thinking as the Swedish coastline came into view, how much I loved seeing the now familiar sight of a Swedish city in the distance. The two countries are so close and similar in many ways, but there are surprising differences even so.

14

Droppsta

Once I'd got the job at Burroughs, it was clear that we would be staying in Sweden for the foreseeable future, and that it wasn't ideal living under the same roof as George and Britta – either for them or for us. As luck would have it, there was a vacant house on the farm – in fact two vacant semi-detached houses, side by side, probably about a hundred years old. They would have been occupied by farm workers in the past, but not lived in for several years. Britta said we could rent one of them if we wanted to. She said the one on the right was in a better state. We went over to have a look at it one day.

It was absolutely beautiful. Stairs up as you walked though the front door, a large kitchen at the front on the right, a living room at the back behind the kitchen, and a small bathroom straight ahead with WC and shower.

Droppsta Gård. We lived in the red house on the left

Upstairs a bedroom in the centre of the space, with the ridge of the roof above, and large storage areas either side of the bedroom, under the sloping roof.

Yes, just perfect. And it looked so right from the outside too – Falu red, with white trim. We'd never lived in a traditional Swedish house before but we knew it was just right for us. We could pretend we were living in a Carl Larsson painting. And it smelt right too – not at all musty, just that wonderful Swedish pine smell. As with many things, there is a Swedish way of building houses: 'this is the way we do it' (a phrase we heard often, in relation to all sorts of things, even the way they cooked a certain dish). The windows and fittings, the doors, the lighting – all just how it was meant to be. And, to top it all, an actual Husqvarna wood stove! George said it needed a bit of attention, but what the hell, there it was in all its glory. A machine to feed us, and to keep us warm – it fed all the radiators.

The rent was very reasonable, and we said, 'Yes please, we'll take it.' And so we were to have our own roof over our heads again. Well not really 'ours', but you know what I mean. It would have been about April by now, and spring was in the air. Most of the snow had melted, and the days were getting longer. It was now fifteen months since we'd left England, and all that time we'd kept on our Nottingham flat, as we didn't know how long we were going to be in Sweden. Extravagant? Not really – the rent was £16 a month, which was cheap even for then. We'd left a lot of stuff there, including some furniture. Now it was time to let the flat go, and bring over what furniture we thought we needed.

I had my full-time job at Burroughs, so we decided that Wendy would take the Mini, and bring back whatever she could fit in the 6 x 4 trailer that George lent us. We didn't actually have a tow-ball on the back of the car, so, no problem, we put the trailer upside-down on the roof-rack. We booked a ticket on our old friend the Swedish Lloyd ferry from Gothenburg to Tilbury. Early one morning I waved goodbye to Wendy as she set off for Gothenburg, 500km away. Not too many motorways in those days, it would have taken a good eight hours to get to Gothenburg.

I resigned myself to a solitary life for a couple of weeks. How would I eat? (Joke). George kindly offered to give me a lift to the train station every day in the Spitfire.

A few hours later that day, a car pulls up outside – it's a blue Mini. Strange. Then a familiar figure appears

– it's Wendy. Oh dear what can the matter be? The car had broken down: the ignition light had come on because the fan belt had broken. Not that uncommon in those days, at least on British cars. She'd only got to Västerås, 100km or so. Better than nearly to Gothenburg, but even so, it had been a traumatic experience for Wendy, including getting a lift with a stranger in the early hours of the morning. And 200km of wasted driving. She came back because she would have missed the ferry sailing that she was booked on. There were only three sailings a week, so she spent the night at home, then set off again early next morning. It would be two weeks before we would see each other again.

Meanwhile, George liked to tinker in his garage, and he was interested in cars – something I knew little about. He drove a Triumph Spitfire Mark III – it was white with a soft top and even I could appreciate its qualities. He decided it needed its valves grinding (I wondered what that meant) so the car was soon up on axle stands, the head came off the engine, and the valves removed. Then he found some grinding paste and started to twirl each valve in the paste. It was a long, exacting process. In my ignorance I thought it strange that he was mending something that wasn't broken. He explained that it was all to do with engine efficiency and smooth running. So I learnt something about engines, and he even let me do a bit of twirling.

On another occasion I'd borrowed George's other car, which he'd had in England and was now on 'Q' plates – UK export plates. I noticed from the tax disc that the plates were expired. I'd been shopping in Märsta, and as I joined the E4 to head home, I slowed right down but failed to stop at the stop sign – I could see the road was clear for a long way. I was getting up to speed when I'm overtaken by an unmarked police car – a Volvo with a portable blue flashing light on the roof. He signalled me to stop. It pulled up in front of me, and two burly men get out. One of them walks over to the driver's side. He doesn't seem surprised to find there's nobody there. Then he sees me on the passenger side. He walks round and shows me his ID. It's always best to stick to English in these situations. His English is good (of course).

'You didn't stop at the stop sign.'

I make my excuses: there wasn't a car in sight. Then he wants to see my ID. I explain that I haven't got my passport on me – which is an offence in itself – you're always supposed to have at least your driving licence on you. I tell him my passport's at home, which isn't far away. He says, 'OK we follow you there.' Well at least he's more concerned with me than the expired plates on the car. I didn't want to get George involved. And I'm sure George doesn't want to get involved either. The cops must be thinking, this is a change from writing speeding tickets. I drive for ten minutes or so up the E4 and take the short track to home, with the unmarked car behind. I leave them at the front door and fetch my UK passport. They flick through it and find my Swedish residence permit. Are they disappointed? They don't appear to be. The talkative one says, 'OK, make sure you stop at stop signs.' I was relieved to get away with a warning; it could have been a hefty fine. And George didn't get done for expired plates either. Which I would have had to pay.

Meanwhile Wendy had made it to Gothenburg safely and in time for the ferry. It was a 36-hour voyage, a long time on your own. Then another 150 miles to Nottingham. The flat was still there, just as we left it all that time ago, no break-ins, no burst water pipes luckily.

We had good friends in Nottingham, and they helped Wendy get a tow-ball fitted, then helped her with the mammoth job of emptying the flat. We had the first and second floors of the house, so a lot of stairs to climb. What it is to be young and fit and strong. Some stuff was taken to a second-hand dealer, other stuff was loaded in the trailer and all over the Mini with a small space for the driver, and the rest to the tip. It would have been an impossible job for one person, so we are still grateful for the help of those good friends. And Wendy was fed and watered too.

The garage had fitted a tow-ball – but no electrical connection. That would have been an even heftier bill, and it was only a one-off trip after all. So – no rear lights, no indicator lights and no brake-lights. Hmmm, very illegal. But Wendy was inventive and came up with an ingenious solution – two sixpenny torches from Asda, attached to the trailer with sticky tape. Brilliant! Here's the final touch – she painted each lens red with a felt-tipped pen. You could just about see a small circle of reddish light – from six feet away. But hey, it would get her home, wouldn't it?

So, a few days later, with some junk still left in the flat, which our friends said they'd get rid of for us, Wendy sets off for faraway Droppsta. A long, long way to go. The car almost as heavy as a Volvo truck, and a weighty unlit trailer behind. The journey back to Tilbury was in day-time luckily, and Wendy got to the safety of the ferry without a hitch. It must have been a huge relief also to be in the comfort of the ship, and maybe to have a cup of coffee and a Prince. You remember Prince? It's a cigarette, not a he. And another 36 hours on the thankfully calm North Sea.

Then the seemingly endless eight hour drive back to Droppsta on deserted Swedish roads. By the time Wendy got back, it was late evening. It was a long time since we'd been together – there was a lot to talk about. I marvelled at her exploits and achievements. She was impressed with the state of the house.

You wouldn't think you could get much furniture in a Mini and a small trailer, but you'd be surprised. There were many little treasures that we hadn't seen for a long time, things that made our house into a home.

Meanwhile George had the bright idea of ripping the wood stove out and checking the plumbing – a major operation. The water pipes would have been there for ever and were very reluctant to unscrew from their fittings on the stove. The stove itself had been bricked in when installed, and that all had to come out. George was one of those blokes who liked to take things apart so he could put them back together again. Or maybe he was right and something did need fixing. In any event when it was all put together again, the stove worked fine, both for cooking and for heating the radiators.

The bathroom also needed some work. The toilet had to be replaced, so we drove down to OBS, the shop that sold everything, and bought a new toilet. I worked out how to install that – a useful bit of experience. The bathroom floor too had to be tiled. We got some new tiles cheap from somewhere. Two lessons I learnt on that project – firstly, large tiles would have been so much quicker and easier to lay than the two-inch tiles I was using; and secondly, whatever you do, make sure you clean up the excess grout immediately – not a week later when it has set firm all over the face of the tiles.

Another of George's talents was teaching English to adults. He had a weekly class at the *folkhögskola* in Sigtuna. He asked Wendy and me if we'd be interested in going along one evening. Sure, we said, we'd love to. We went on separate occasions. The time I went there were about eight people in the classroom. Right at the start George introduces me and then he asks me if I would like to tell them something. I suppose I should have thought about that beforehand. Also I should have got an idea of their proficiency in English. As it was, I just saw these expectant faces looking at me. On the spur of the moment, I thought I'd tell them a joke. Not a good idea considering that you needed a good command of English vocabulary to get this particular joke. It was so awful I still remember it. There was this man who wants to buy a parrot. He goes into the parrot shop, and there are parrots on two rungs, one higher than the other. The assistant explains that the parrots on the top row are more expensive than the ones on the bottom row. 'Why's that?', asks the man. 'Because they're on hire purchase (higher perches).' Well, you should have seen the reaction. Reader, there was none. Faces like stunned mullets. It was the original dead parrot sketch. Of course – they'd hardly understood a word I'd said. George handled it well and got me off the hook.

Wendy did a much better job than me. In fact she stood in for George on a couple of occasions. It was the first of several TEFL courses she later gave, both in Sweden and in Holland, and the very beginning of her passion for adult community education.

Our living room in Droppsta

We lived happily in Droppsta for a year or more. The snow melted and the spring came. We got milk and eggs from the farm next door – we were always treated so well by Britta's family. Britta's brother and his wife ran the farm, and they had two small children. Britta's parents had retired and still lived in their own house on the farm. Wendy would be invited for *fika* by Britta's mother. We were grateful to them for letting us rent their lovely little house.

I went off to Burroughs on the train every day. Wendy made our new home a wonderful place to come back to every day. She chopped logs in the shed. She lit the stove

That 70s look

and baked in the oven, and she helped out on the farm. The house smelt of Swedish pine and bread. She had a beautiful young cat – jet black, lithe, shy. Her name, for some reason, was *Tuggummi* (chewing gum) *Lisa*.

Summer came, the days grew long and we luxuriated in *sommaren*. Mostly we were happy to just *be* in our cottage in the fields. Helena and Vic would sometimes visit us, and we'd drink tea in the garden, smoke a Prince and talk about the old times – last year.

We found some old, but stylish, bits of furniture. Britta's family lent us the beautiful white pine desk in the photo. On one occasion there was an auction in Odensala, a neighbouring village. It was in the main street, by the side of the road, with just a handful of local people there.

There were some marvellous old Swedish artefacts going under the (imagined) hammer – probably the contents of a deceased estate. One item in particular caught Wendy's eye – a cast-iron waffle iron, heavy and old but not at all rusty, clearly recently used. The bidding started at one krone (ten pence) and rose rapidly to six kronor. Wendy really wanted it. '*Sju*' she called out. Seven – a brave move. Why brave? As anyone trying to learn Swedish knows, *sj* is the hardest consonant to pronounce: it's something like the English 'sh' , but it's not that. But no heads turned, so she'd said it well. She could have taken the easy way out and bid eight kronor – anyone can say *åtta*. The story has a happy ending: that bid clinched the deal, and she'd saved a krone. And what's more, we still use that *våffeljärn* to this day.

Which reminds me of a well-known Swedish tongue-twister: *Sju sjösjuka sjömän sköttes av sju sköna sjuksköterskor.* It's easier in English: Seven seasick seamen were cared for by seven beautiful nurses.

Something else we needed was kitchen chairs. We got those from IKEA – they were fold-up and wooden, painted black, and they were called Klapp. They were a giveaway price – less than the price of two packets of cigarettes, I remember thinking at the time. And those we also have fifty years later. I see IKEA have the same type of chair in their catalogue today, except it's called Terje. What was wrong with Klapp?

Every now and then we went into Stockholm, the city on the water, an old familiar friend by now. We'd catch up with Helena there too. Sometimes we'd all go to our old stamping ground, the Tudor Arms, drink a Tuborg and have a game of arrers on the dartboard. Or we'd enjoy a wonderful real pizza in another familiar haunt, Pizzeria Capri on Nybrogatan – with a glass of strega to follow.

We were happy then. We didn't travel afar – we didn't feel the need to, and we couldn't have afforded to anyway. Air travel was so expensive in those days. And, with one exception, nobody visited us from the UK – probably for the same reason. Scandinavia seemed like a mythical faraway place when you lived in England – and yet it's only two hours on a plane – much nearer than the Mediterranean for example.

Our one visitor was Wendy's nephew Dean, who was eleven. Dean is Wendy's sister Jill's son. His father Rupe was a top ice hockey player in England. He'd played for Great Britain in the Winter Olympics, and in all the ice hockey playing countries – Canada, Russia, Scandinavia. So Dean had heard from his dad a bit about Sweden. Britta had a son, Johan, of a similar age to Dean. They got on well together, and made little of the language divide. One day Dean appears in full ice hockey uniform, complete with helmet, stick and skates. We have a photo to prove it. No matter that it was high summer. He looked the part: ice hockey was clearly in his genes.

Johan and Dean

Soon winter was upon us – there was no Guy Fawkes party at George and Britta's this year as all the SPL people had been scattered around Europe. As Christmas 1972 approached, we'd saved up enough to fly back to London to stay with Wendy's parents for a family celebration.

We got back to Droppsta early in 1973. It was then that our first thoughts arose about leaving Sweden and going back home. We had a wonderful life in Sweden, but maybe we had the feeling that we were a bit cut off, and that there was more for us to explore and discover in the big wide world. It could have been my eternal wanderlust but luckily I didn't have to convince Wendy that it was time to move on.

I talked to Ingmar at Burroughs about our plans, and he was surprised that I was leaving. I asked him if he would give me a reference, and an introduction to Burroughs UK, who were the obvious place to look for a job. He wrote me a nice letter 'to whom it may concern'. Even though, as you may remember, I wasn't officially on Burroughs' books. I don't think there were any repercussions.

And so, in April 1973, we said goodbye to our friends in Droppsta. By the time we'd loaded up the Mini to suspension overloading point, it became clear that there was just enough room for the driver, but not for a passenger. I volunteered to drive, and Wendy said she'd get the train and ferry. She went to OBS and bought the largest suitcase she could find, and packed it to bulging. She had an arduous journey of several days and finally got back to her folks in London. The next day I headed west to Gothenburg and the Tilbury ferry. Maybe I should have suggested that Wendy drive and I'd get the train and ferry.

England seemed very provincial after our two years away. Maybe that's an unfriendly way of saying it was friendlier than Sweden. I had to get used to saying please and thank you all the time. Once or twice I forgot and got some disapproving looks.

There had been some changes in the meantime: all the money was funny. The UK had gone decimal, and there were new coins that we'd never seen before. But one thing hadn't changed: the pubs and real ale. Those things I was happy to have on every street corner.

Looking back, we were privileged to have grown up in the 60s and now the early years of the 70s, a vibrant, stable, prosperous and peaceful time. Those adjectives need some qualification: stable in most of Britain and all of Sweden, prosperous for many people, peaceful in most of Europe. Things were about to become less stable with the oil crisis just around the corner, and industrial unrest and the three-day week in Britain.

We weren't homesick for Sweden, which seems strange in retrospect as we'd been so happy there. It was probably that England now seemed like a big new adventure, especially as we'd decided to settle down in a part of the country that we didn't know at all. Also we were closer to our families; I had been remiss in my lack of communication with my parents and my brother Ian and my sisters Jane and Lizzie. (I've tried to make up for that in later years.)

We lived first in a rented flat in Rottingdean, East Sussex. I soon got a job with Burroughs in Shoreham-by-Sea, just down the road. And Wendy got a good job in IT in Lewes. The ferry from Newhaven to Dieppe was a plus point in favour of the area. We looked around to buy a house in Brighton, a young and trendy city that appealed to us. But there had been a property boom and prices were just out of our reach.

Early in 1974 we ended up moving to Sydenham (Dulwich borders!), an unfashionable suburb in South London, where house prices were lower. There were plenty of IT jobs in London and we were able to buy our first property. But that is a new chapter in the story; or rather, a different book, should it ever be written.

Postscript

Wendy and I formed a love of Sweden in those two and a bit years. So much so that we have been back there many times since. We still love to be there, especially as we now live on the other side of the world. Wendy put it very well in one of our recent blog posts:

What is it about this place that makes our hearts sing?
Is it:
- *the landscape backed by pine forests and edged with wild flowers*
- *little red cottages with white paintwork*
- *picking wild strawberries*
- *the taste of really new potatoes with sill (marinated herring)*
- *the wonderfully long days: sunrise at 4am and sunset at 10pm*
- *that special Scandinavian design and style*
- *cinnamon buns in an old-fashioned, yet stylish, konditori?*

Answer: all of the above and much more!

From shearwood.wordpress.com, the post dated July 21st 2019. You can read more about our travels there.

By 1999 we had lived in the Netherlands as well as in England, and we'd embarked on another adventure – we'd emigrated to Australia eleven years previously. Our family had increased by two, with Helen now aged twenty-three and Martin aged twenty. One of the many good things about Australia is long-service leave. That's three months of paid leave after you have worked for an employer for a certain number of years. Nowadays it's usually ten or fifteen years, but back then, for both Wendy and for me, it was only seven years. What a winner that was. We eagerly looked forward to our three months of freedom, which fell due in 1999 and, guess what, it could only mean a long trip to Europe.

And that, of course, included Sweden. Which brought with it a nostalgic return to Stockholm and to Droppsta. We soon found where Britta was living in a nearby town, and it was lovely to see her again – after twenty-six years. But she had some sad news – George had died a few years before, at a relatively young age. He'd had the beginnings of MS when we left in 1973.

Britta took us to see the farm, and our house looked exactly the same as it did when we lived there. It was

Graham, Wendy, Martin, Helen, Darren

a thrill to be there again after all those years. The old schoolhouse looked the same, but with new residents. There had been other changes at the farm: now they offered farm-stay holidays and there was a farm shop, as well as their farming business. Agriculture in Europe generally now favoured farms of a huge size – at least that was my interpretation.

In 2008 the idea was sparked that it was possible that we as a family could buy a *stuga* (summerhouse) in Sweden. As mentioned earlier, summerhouses are often old, a hundred years or more, built from pine logs, painted in *fururöd* (dark red) and they are dotted all over the countryside. Often they have been in the same family for many generations.

Our son Martin had been surfing the web and came across *stugor* for sale in a very reasonable price range, especially when divided amongst the five of us. From being a fanciful dream, reality became a bit closer when Martin and I were in the UK at the end of 2008 and we decided that it would be fun to actually go over to Sweden and check out some houses that were for sale. So we did.

We chose the south-east corner of the country, thinking that would be a bit more remote and peaceful than the slightly busier south-west corner. We booked into a hotel in Växjö for a week, hired a car, and chose five areas in which to look at two or three houses in each, a different area each day. We made appointments with estate agents, who must have wondered if these two Australians were fair dinkum, viewing properties on the other side of the world in winter. But they showed us some wonderful properties. All the family felt that it had to be a red house, as you will remember, so we only looked at red houses.

On one of our viewing days we were in Blekinge, a small county in the far south-east corner of the country. We viewed a house in a small village called Stora Silpinge that ticked all the boxes, as they say. It was a chilly day, being November, but the sun was shining, and the house and the village and the area were just stunning – straight out of a fairytale. After the viewing Martin and I drove a few kilometres on to the next village where there was a small farm shop. We rang Wendy. We said we'd found it. She must have been surprised, to say the least. We sent the link to the website to Wendy, Helen and Darren, our son-in-law. They all said, 'Let's buy it'. We put in an offer and it was accepted.

Settlement was in February 2009. All five of us were eager to go and visit our new property. We knew the weather would be beautiful in late spring, so we booked our flights for May. When the happy day arrived, we flew into Copenhagen, and picked up a hire car. We drove over the beautiful Öresund bridge, and were soon in the green fields and on the empty roads of Sweden. It was only a leisurely three-hour drive to Silpinge. And there she was, resplendent in the spring sunshine, waiting for her new owners. For Martin and me it was a happy reunion. And Wendy, Helen and Darren gave their seal of approval to their unseen purchase – but then I knew they would.

We spent a memorable three weeks there, throwing open the windows, letting in the fresh air, doing minor repairs, painting, scrubbing, mowing the grass, listening to the birdsong and occasionally the silence. It wasn't all roses: the well had dried up and we had to get a new well built – but we soon got that sorted with the help of some local expertise. We had an ample water supply from then on.

There was lots of space for all five of us, and we soon fell into the rhythm of life in the country. We knew that our decision and investment had been the the right one.

Over the following few summers, we came back – not all together again – but the peace and quiet were always the same. Wendy and I got to know several of the people who lived in the village, and they welcomed us into village activities. *Midsommar* was the celebration it always was, and we were happy to help with the preparations – picking wild flowers and silver birch branches to decorate the midsummer pole, and erecting the side-show stalls. Throughout the summer there would be a *brasafton* (barbeque) once a month on a Friday evening, at a different family's house each time. We were welcomed there too, and people were so patient in accepting our willing attempts to remember some words of Swedish from forty years previously.

When none of us were there in the summer, we rented the house out on short-term holiday lets. We were lucky enough to meet Silke who became our local agent when we were far away. Now we could share the pleasure of living there with other, unseen, guests. Our guest book told us how much they had enjoyed the experience.

But the time came, after nine years, when we decided that it was time to let go our piece of Swedish heaven: it was a commitment to maintain it from so far away. So we put it on the market – with Tobias the same estate agent we had bought it through originally. Before long we had a reasonable offer and it was bought by another family. There was a mixture of emotions about letting it go, as can be imagined.

In 2019 Wendy and I were in the area and we took the opportunity to visit our village and drive by our cottage. We were happy to see windows open to the summer sunshine, tables and chairs and toys in the garden: clear evidence of a young family living there, and enjoying what was there to be enjoyed. We stopped for a few moments at the end of the drive and sat in silence, but we didn't knock on the door. As we drove away, I didn't turn to look at Wendy.

Till våra vänner i Sverige

I Stockholm hälsar vi till Helena o. Nancy.

I Kvibille hälsar vi till Björn o. Kerstin.

I Silpinge hälsar vi till Inga-Stina o. hennes familj, Roy o. Gerd, Hans o. Agneta, Yngve o. Linda, Birger o. Inger, Roger o. Anneli.

I Röaby hälsar vi till Heike Tlatlik.

I Listerby hälsar vi till Silke Peter.

I Lyckeby hälsar vi till Tobias Malving.

I Saxemora hälsar vi till Inge Petersson.

www.ingramcontent.com/pod-product-compliance
Lightning Source LLC
Chambersburg PA
CBHW070256010526
44107CB00056B/2476